START WITHOUT PERMISSION

HOW TO BUILD POWER, MOMENTUM, AND SUCCESS WHEN NO ONE IS OPENING DOORS

PHOEBE A. BRYANT

Copyright © 2026 by Phoebe A. Bryant

All rights are reserved, and no part of this publication may be reproduced, distributed, or transmitted in any manner, whether through photocopying, recording, or any other electronic or mechanical methods, without the explicit prior written permission of the publisher. This restriction applies to any form or means of reproduction or distribution.

Exceptions to this rule include brief quotations that may be incorporated into critical reviews, as well as certain other noncommercial uses that are allowed by copyright law. Any such usage must adhere to the specified conditions and permissions outlined by the copyright holder.

Book Design by HMDPublishing.com

CONTENTS

Find Your Starting Point. 5
Introduction. 9

PART I - THE UNDERDOG ADVANTAGE

Chapter 1. Build In Public Before You're Ready 15
Chapter 2. Prove It With Work, Not Words 29
Chapter 3. Build Your Own Door When They Lock You Out . 42

PART II - PROOF IN MOTION

Chapter 4. Teach What You Know, Multiply What You Build . 53
Chapter 5. Turn Rejection Into Redirection 64
Chapter 6. Find Your People And Build Together 80

PART III - CREATE YOUR OWN DOOR

Chapter 7. Stack Small Wins Into Big Breakthroughs . . .97
Chapter 8. Know Your Worth And Name Your Price 111
Chapter 9. Build Your Own Stage When They Won't
              Give You The Mic. 125

PART IV - LEGACY MODE

Chapter 10. Master The Rules Before You Rewrite Them . . 140

Chapter 11. Build Receipts That Silence Doubt. 155

Afterword **169**

Acknowledgements **171**

About The Author. **173**

Notes **174**

FIND YOUR STARTING POINT

This book builds on lessons, but you don't have to start at Chapter 1. Begin where you are.

Where Are You Right Now?	Start
I have an idea but haven't started yet.	Chapter 1
I keep getting told "this won't work" or "you don't belong here".	Chapter 2
I'm building but losing motivation or questioning if it matters.	Chapter 3
I've built something that works, but if I'm the only one doing it—it doesn't scale.	Chapter 4
I keep getting rejected and I'm not sure whether to keep trying or pivot.	Chapter 5
I'm doing okay alone but wonder if I need a partner to go further.	Chapter 6
I've been building for years with small wins but no big breakthrough.	Chapter 7
I've built value but struggle to get paid what I'm worth.	Chapter 8
I keep hearing "no" and wonder when to quit vs. when to persist.	Chapter 9
I want to change or improve systems in my field.	Chapter 10
I'm building publicly but facing lots of rejection from gatekeepers or investors.	Chapter 11

Still Not Sure Where to Start?

Default to Chapter One. Starting before you are ready is the universal first move. Whether you are in your first year or your fifteenth, there is always a first version you could launch today that you are waiting to perfect. Read Chapter One. Take one action from it this week. Then come back and choose your next chapter.

A Note on Reading Strategically

This book gives you eleven role models and forty-four principles. You do not need all forty-four right now. You need the three to five that speak to your current challenge. Your situation will change. When it does, a different chapter will suddenly feel urgent. That is when you come back and read it.

This book is not meant to be read once and shelved. It is a companion that meets you at different stages of your journey.

AUTHOR'S NOTE

I wrote this book because I was tired of reading stories that inspired me but never included me.

The entrepreneur, business, and self-development section is filled with brilliant lessons from people who had built empires, made millions, or revolutionized their industries. I loved those stories. They motivated me for a moment. But somewhere between the lines, I realized something: they were never written for someone who looked like me.

The characters who looked like me, thought like me, or started where I started were missing. Most of the stories began with access: the right networks, the right mentors, the right capital. But many of us start without any of those advantages. What we have instead is resilience shaped by a reality many authors never acknowledge: the invisible weight of unconscious bias.

This truth sits underneath the surface of so many professional spaces. It sounds like you are not the right fit. It looks like being passed over for a promotion that never had your name in mind. It is being asked to prove what others are simply trusted to know.

I am not interested in assigning blame. I am interested in what happens when we stop pretending the playing field is level and start building in spite of it.

In this book, you will meet innovators, creators, and leaders who were underestimated and used that underestimation as fuel. Their stories prove that brilliance is universal, even if opportunity is not. You will see how they learned, failed, pivoted, and built momentum through strategy, not luck. You will discover the framework that connects them all: how to break through barriers not by asking for entry, but by showing that you already belong.

This book is for the people who have worked hard, played by the rules, and still find themselves on the outside looking in. It is for those who have been told they are talented but not quite ready. It is for those waiting for a title, a gatekeeper, or validation that never seems to come.

If you have ever been underestimated, overlooked, or told to wait your turn, this book is for you. If you have felt invisible in rooms you worked hard to enter, if you are tired of waiting for permission that never comes, this is your moment.

You do not need a green light to begin. You only need the courage to start.

— Phoebe A. Bryant

INTRODUCTION

The First Door I Built

When I was twenty-four, I left everything familiar for something I could not quite define.

Atlanta was home, warm, busy, and filled with people who looked like me. But I wanted to move up in the company I worked for, a major bank with a management internship that promised opportunity.

So I packed my car and drove north to Newark, Delaware.

The moment I stepped inside headquarters, I felt the air change. I could count the number of Black people I saw on one hand, including myself. The silence around me whispered, "*You do not belong here.*"

That first night, I called my mom in tears. She listened, then said the words I needed most: *"You're strong enough to see this through. Remember why you're there."*

So, I stayed.

I was placed in the IT department, in a role I did not ask for and did not understand. Two weeks later, the internship program director found me and said there had been a mistake. I was supposed to be somewhere else. But before I could pack my things, my IT manager intervened. He wanted me to stay.

I did not know it then, but that moment would change everything.

That summer turned into a career, one where I would almost always be the "only one in the room." The only woman. The only Black person. The only one without a computer science degree.

I remember the first time someone asked me, "What kind of money do you see yourself making in ten years?"

I said maybe forty thousand dollars. I was young and hopeful. My manager looked at me and said, *"You are reaching too high."*

That feeling, of being told to dream smaller, became familiar. In meetings, my questions were met with impatience. My ambitions, with polite disbelief. I learned early that if I wanted a path forward, I would have to build it myself.

So I did.

I learned the capabilities of building systems and infrastructure. I took the projects no one wanted. When something broke, I fixed it. When no one volunteered, I raised my hand. I stacked proof until my work spoke louder than my title. And somewhere between frustration and persistence, I stopped waiting for permission.

That moment, that shift, is what this book is about.

This is not a book of motivational speeches or empty affirmations. It is a field guide for doers, for people who know they have more to give but are stuck waiting for someone else to say "yes."

It is about stacking small wins until they become undeniable. Building proof when no one is offering you a platform. And learning to stop knocking on closed doors because you can build your own.

In these pages, you will meet people who did exactly that.

Some started with nothing but a camera and a story. Others built businesses from kitchen tables or laptops on borrowed Wi Fi. None of them waited to be ready. They started where they were, with what they had.

Each chapter breaks their journey down into practical sections: *Reader Transitions, Play by Plays, Power Moves, Mind Traps, and Modern Reflections.*

Their stories are not just inspiration; they are instruction. The truth is, you do not need another pep talk. You need a plan.

A way to take what you have right now, your ideas, your resilience, your energy, and turn it into forward motion.

That is what *Start Without Permission* is built to do.

So if you have ever been told to wait your turn, to blend in, or to lower your expectations, let this be the last time you do. This is not your invitation. It is your reminder that you never needed one.

Start without permission.

PART ONE
THE UNDERDOG ADVANTAGE

Every disadvantage hides an advantage — if you know how to use it.

We tend to think the people who win started ahead.

They had better mentors, better timing, better resources. But when you look closely, that is rarely true. The people who create change, the ones who rewrite the rules, almost always start behind.

They do not begin with privilege. They begin with pressure.

They do not inherit platforms. They build them. They do not wait to be discovered. They make themselves impossible to ignore.

That is the underdog advantage.

It is the energy that comes from being overlooked, counted out, or told no. It is what happens when you realize that no one is coming to give you permission, and that your best chance at winning is to start anyway.

Starting from behind allows you to see things differently. You notice what others overlook. You move with intention. You develop resourcefulness because you have to. After that, every barrier becomes a blueprint. Every no becomes data. Every setback becomes a test run for your next move.

The women in this book did not start with certainty. They started with frustration, curiosity, or necessity. Some were broke. Some were ignored. Some were told, directly, that people like them did not belong in the rooms they wanted to enter.

They did not argue back. They built proof.

And in doing so, they discovered something every underdog eventually learns. Disadvantage is not your weakness. It is your weapon.

When no one expects you to win, you have nothing to protect. You can take risks others are too comfortable to take. You can be bolder, scrappier, faster. You can fail publicly and learn faster than people who hide behind titles or funding or privilege.

That is how momentum begins.

In this first part of the book, you will see how starting before you are ready can become your superpower. You will witness how showing up imperfectly can attract opportunity faster than waiting for polish, and how to use your current position, no matter how small, unseen, or temporary, as the foundation for something undeniable.

The stories that follow are not about luck. They are about leverage. Each woman turned what she did not have into proof of what she could do. They built in public. They learned out loud. They found their audience by being real, not perfect.

And that is your challenge, too.

Do not waste your underdog energy trying to look established. Use it to build something extraordinary from where you are. Your advantage is not in what you have been given. It is in what you have survived, what you have learned, and what you can build from it.

Every disadvantage hides an advantage — if you know how to use it.

CHAPTER 1

BUILD IN PUBLIC BEFORE YOU'RE READY

"Don't wait for perfect. Start where you are, with what you have. The proof comes from doing."
Issa Rae.

Every movement starts with someone deciding to stop hiding. There is a moment, small and quiet, when they choose to begin even though the world is not watching. They do not wait for better tools, a bigger following, or perfect timing. They use what they have, where they are, and they share it before it feels finished.

That decision, to be visible before you are ready, is what separates people who talk about their ideas from the ones who build them.

Opening Scene

In 2011, Issa Rae had a camera, some friends, and a story nobody in Hollywood wanted to tell. She didn't wait for a studio deal or an agent or permission. She made *Awkward Black Girl* in her apartment and posted it on YouTube.

The first episodes weren't perfect—the lighting was uneven, the sound had issues—but they were real. And real was exactly what millions of viewers had been waiting for. By 2015, HBO came calling. By 2016, *Insecure* premiered to critical acclaim. By 2020, Issa had built a production company, published a *New York Times* bestseller, and changed what stories get told on television.

She didn't wait to be ready. She started before she was ready. And that made all the difference.

This is how you begin.

Reader's Transition

This is where it begins for all of us, the uncomfortable first version, the shaky first try, the uncertain start that nobody applauds at first. Some people wait for gatekeepers to say yes. They wait for the right connections, for someone to discover them, for permission to create. They are still waiting.

You do not need industry experts to greenlight your show, a publisher to approve your book, or investors to fund your new business. You need an idea, desire, and the courage to share something before you are ready. The moment you decide to create before you are qualified is the moment you begin to separate yourself from the crowd still waiting for the greenlight.

When you build in public, three things happen. First, you learn faster because real people give you real feedback. Second, you build an audience before you need one. Third, you create proof that bypasses all the gatekeepers. The world that once said no one wants this becomes the world that demands more of it, because you did not wait for permission. You gave it to yourself.

This pattern appears across every industry. In healthcare, it's launching a patient newsletter before writing the book. In consulting, it's piloting your program with three clients before building the full offering. In food, it's testing recipes at farmers' markets before opening the restaurant.

Issa's story shows that your version 0.1 —the messy, imperfect, but *honest* start—isn't the weakest part of your journey. It's the foundation that makes everything else possible. As you read Issa's story, ask yourself: What would my "Version 0.1" look like—the smallest, messiest version of my idea that I could launch this week?

Origin

January 12, 1985. Los Angeles, California.

Jo Issa Rae Diop was born to parents who met while studying in France, her mother Delyna, a teacher from Louisiana, and her father Abdoulaye, a pediatrician from Senegal. Issa was one of five children, her name a combination of her grandmothers' names, Joyce and Isseu.

When Issa was young, the family moved to Dakar, Senegal, where her father planned to build a hospital. She attended a West African school as the only American kid there. Already, she did not quite fit. Then the hospital plan collapsed. Someone scammed her father, and the family lost a significant amount of money. They moved back to the United States, this time to Potomac, Maryland, a wealthy suburb.

In Potomac, Issa attended a gifted and talented elementary school where she was often one of the few Black kids in her classes. She did swim team and street hockey, things her older brothers teased her about, saying she was "too white." She wrote later that being Black there "was easy" because she did not have to think about her race much. But she did not fully fit in. Too Black for her white peers, too white for her Black family.

Sixth grade. View Park-Windsor Hills, South Los Angeles.

The family moved again, this time to a predominantly Black neighborhood. Everything changed. At her new middle school, kids teased her for "talking white," the way she spoke, the things she was interested in, her experiences from Maryland. She was an outsider again. Different environment, same feeling.

At King Drew Magnet High School, where most students were Black and Latino, she joined the drama department and finally found something, a space where being different was not wrong, where she could tell stories, where the portrayals of Black life felt more authentic and more three dimensional. But the feeling of not quite fitting in never left. It became part of who she was.

2003-2007. Stanford University.

Issa studied African and African American Studies while writing and directing plays. She made a mockumentary web series called *Dorm Diaries*—nothing big, just experimenting and learning what she was good at. She graduated in 2007 with her degree, ready to take on the world.

The world was not ready for her.

Play by Play

2007-2011. Post-college.

Issa struggled. Hard. She worked odd jobs, considered law school and business school, but neither felt right. She knew she wanted to create and tell stories, but networks kept giving her the same answer when she pitched web series ideas about everyday Black life: "There is no audience for this. These stories are too niche. Nobody wants to watch this."

She developed a pilot for ABC, but to get it made, she had to compromise and change her vision to make it more broadly appealing. ABC passed anyway. By 2011, four years out of college, Issa was struggling financially, working jobs she did not care about, and watching her creative dreams die slowly. She was frustrated, angry, and tired of hearing no.

She thought, If TV will not make the stories I want to tell, I will make them myself. She did not have money, connections, or professional equipment. But she had a camera, friends, and a story. And she had YouTube.

February 3, 2011.

Issa launched *The Misadventures of Awkward Black Girl* on YouTube. The first episode, "The Stop Sign," was low budget. The lighting was not perfect, the production was not polished, but it was real, funny, and hers. She played J, an awkward Black woman navigating uncomfortable professional and personal situations, a character who was uncomfortable in her own skin, never quite sure how to act, always feeling out of place. It was Issa's life on screen.

She uploaded the episode with no marketing budget and no PR team, just a YouTube link and hope. People watched. A lot of people. The first episode got over 240,000 views, and comments poured in: "This is my life." "I have never seen myself on screen before." "Where has this been?" Women everywhere felt seen, especially Black women who had been told they were too this or not enough that, women who felt awkward and did not fit the stereotypes.

Issa and her producer Tracy Oliver kept making episodes, but they ran out of money. They launched a Kickstarter campaign with a goal of $30,000. By August 11, 2011, they had raised $56,269 from 1,960 backers. People did not just want the show. They wanted to fund it, support it, and be part of it. Later episodes consistently pulled over 100,000 views, and the show spread through social media, blogs, and word of mouth.

By September 2011, the Facebook page had nearly 17,000 fans.

2012.

Pharrell Williams noticed. His creative collective "I am OTHER" picked up *Awkward Black Girl* for season two. Now it wasn't just a web series. It was a movement.

2014.

Issa's YouTube channel had accumulated more than 25 million views total. Hollywood noticed. Shonda Rhimes, one of the most powerful producers in TV, reached out. Issa developed another project for ABC, but again, ABC passed. Still, she kept building and started developing a new series with comedian Larry Wilmore.

2015.

HBO picked up the pilot for the new series, called *Insecure*. This time, Issa had leverage—she wasn't unknown anymore. She had 25 million YouTube views, a proven audience, and proof that people wanted her stories. HBO gave her creative control to make the show she wanted, keep the authentic voice, and cast the people she wanted. She didn't have to compromise her vision this time because she'd already proved the audience existed.

Breakthrough

Fall 2016.

Insecure premiered on HBO. It was everything *Awkward Black Girl* was, but bigger—better production, deeper storytelling, the same authentic voice. Critics loved it. Audiences loved it. The show resonated the same way the web series did because it was real, honest, and showed Black life in all its awkward, messy, beautiful complexity.

2016-2021.

Insecure ran for five seasons, and the awards piled up: multiple NAACP Image Awards for Outstanding Comedy Series and Outstanding Actress, 14 Emmy nominations including Outstanding Comedy Series with one win in 2020, three Golden Globe nominations for Best Actress, a Peabody Award in 2017, a Satellite Award win in 2019, and AFI Top 10 Television Programs recognition in 2017 and 2018.

Issa Rae became a name, a brand, a powerhouse. But it all started with a YouTube video she made in 2011 because nobody would give her permission to tell her story.

2021-Present.

After *Insecure* ended, Issa didn't stop. She started her own production company, Hoorae, and produced *Sweet Life: Los Angeles* (2021), *Rap Sh!t* (2022-2023), *Project Greenlight: A New Generation* (2023) mentoring female filmmakers and *Seen & Heard: The History of Black Television* (2025). She executive produced *A Black Lady Sketch Show* (2019-2023) and guest starred in *Black Mirror* (2025).

From a web series made with borrowed equipment to one of the most influential creators in television. From "there's no audience for this" to creating the audience herself, then creating shows for that audience, then creating a production company that creates opportunities for others. That's not luck. That's what happens when you stop waiting for permission and build in public.

Power Moves

1. Start before you're ready

Issa did not wait until she had perfect equipment, professional training, Hollywood connections, or funding. She started with what she had: a camera, friends, and a story. The first episodes of Awkward Black Girl were not polished, but they were real, and real is what people connected with.

Waiting until you are ready is how you never start. Starting before you are ready is how you learn. You do not learn to swim by reading about swimming, you learn by getting in the water, awkwardly making mistakes and getting better. Every public post, video, or project is practice that teaches you something and makes you better.

By the time HBO called, Issa had already made dozens of episodes. She had already learned what worked, what her audience wanted, and what stories resonated. She did not need to guess. She had data.

2. Use feedback as data, not judgment

When you build in public, people will comment. Some feedback will sting, some will be harsh, and some will be trolls. But some will be gold. When multiple people say the same thing, pay attention, that is a pattern, that is data.

Issa's audience told her what they loved: authentic Black characters, awkward moments, real struggles. They told her what they wanted more of: certain storylines, specific characters. That feedback shaped Insecure. By the time she pitched HBO, she knew exactly what her audience wanted because they had been telling her for years.

Listen for patterns. Ignore the noise. Use what helps. Leave what does not.

3. Be real over polished

People don't follow perfect. They follow real. *Awkward Black Girl* wasn't a professionally produced show—the lighting was uneven; the sound wasn't perfect—but it was honest. Issa didn't try to be someone else. She was herself: awkward, funny, real. That authenticity became her brand and why millions of people felt seen. She wasn't pretending. She was just being herself loudly and publicly.

When you share your real process—the wins, the fails, the messy middle—you build trust. People see you're human, see you're trying, and see themselves in you. That's what makes them care: not perfection, but connection.

4. Build your proof publicly

The biggest advantage of building in public? You create proof that bypasses gatekeepers. When Issa pitched her ideas in 2007, networks said "there's no audience." When she pitched in 2015, she had 25 million YouTube views. She had proof. The audience already existed, and she'd built it herself.

That proof gave her leverage. HBO couldn't say "no one wants this" when millions of people were already watching. Every video you post, every project you share, every piece of work you put out publicly—it's proof. Proof you can create, proof people care, proof the audience exists.

Stack enough proof, and you don't need permission anymore. You have leverage.

Mind Trap

The Perfection Mind Trap: Waiting until you're ready (and never starting)

Here is what stops most people from building in public: they think, "It is not good enough yet. I need better equipment. I need more training. I need to be more prepared." So they wait, perfect, plan, and prepare. And they never start.

Why does this happen? Because your brain is trying to protect you from judgment, failure, and embarrassment. It tells you, "If you share this before it is perfect, people will see your flaws. They will judge you. They will think you are not good enough." So you keep polishing, improving, and waiting for the moment when it is finally ready. But that moment never comes because perfect does not exist.

The truth? Imperfect and public beats perfect and private. Every time.

Issa's first episodes were not perfect. The lighting was bad, the production was rough, but they were out there. People could watch them, react to them, and share them. If she had waited until they were perfect, she would still be waiting, and Insecure would never exist.

When you share before you are ready, most people overlook the flaws you worry about. They are paying attention to the content, the story, the message. The people who do notice? Some will criticize, and that is data, use it to improve version two. Some will be trolls, ignore them, they are not your audience. And some, the right people, will appreciate the honesty, connect with the realness, and become fans.

The fix is changing your definition of ready. You are not ready when it is perfect, you are ready when it is honest.

You are not ready when you have professional equipment, you are ready when you have something to say.

You are not ready when you are not scared, you are ready when you do it anyway.

Issa was probably nervous posting that first episode. She probably saw every flaw, every imperfection, every reason it was not ready. But she posted it anyway. And 240,000 people watched it. And her career began.

Your rough draft might be exactly what someone needs to see. Your imperfect project might be the proof you need to get the next opportunity. But only if you share it.

Stop waiting for perfect. Start building for real.

Modern Reflection

When Issa Rae launched *Awkward Black Girl* in 2011, YouTube was different, social media was different, and the creator economy barely existed. There were some successful YouTubers, but web series were still experimental, and the path from YouTube to mainstream success was unclear. Issa was a pioneer who proved that the path existed.

Now, in 2025 and 2026, everything has changed. The tools are better. Cameras are in everyone's pocket, editing software is free or cheap, and you can shoot, edit, and upload a video in hours. The platforms are more mature, offering YouTube, TikTok, Instagram, LinkedIn, Substack, and podcasts, giving everyone multiple options for where to build. The audience is bigger, with billions of people online and niche audiences of millions, making it easier to find your people. The creator economy is real, with people building full time careers on platforms and making millions from YouTube ads, Patreon, sponsorships, courses, and newsletters.

What that means for you: You have no excuse not to start. Issa started with borrowed equipment in 2011. You have a phone camera that is better than professional equipment from 2011. Issa had to figure out YouTube alone. You have tutorials for everything, communities, courses, and templates. Issa could not monetize easily at first. You have more monetization options than ever.

The barrier is not access anymore. It is courage.

But some things have not changed. You still have to do the work, show up consistently, and be real, not perfect. Building in public still works, maybe better than ever, because algorithms reward consistency, community rewards authenticity, and the internet rewards people who show up and share.

The advantage of building in public now: You can get feedback faster by posting a video and seeing responses within hours. You can test ideas cheaper by trying ten different concepts, seeing which resonates, and doubling down. You can find your audience directly with no gatekeepers and no networks saying there is no audience. Your audience can find you right now. You can monetize earlier. As soon as you have a small following, you can make money through Patreon, sponsorships, products, and services.

Here is what has not changed: The gatekeepers still exist. TV networks, publishers, studios, investors. But you do not need them to start. You can build your proof first, then use that proof to get through the gates like Issa did. Or you can skip the gates entirely, build your audience, make your living, and keep creative control. Many creators do.

The power has shifted from institutions to individuals, from gatekeepers to creators. Issa was early to figure this out. You are right on time.

Issa Rae proved something crucial: you do not need permission to start. You need a camera, a story, and the courage to share it before it is perfect.

But starting is not always about creating something new. Sometimes it is about entering a space where you are not supposed to belong. Issa walked into digital media, a relatively open frontier. But what happens when the door you want to walk through is locked, when the industry you want to enter does not want you there?

That is where Patrice Banks found herself. And instead of knocking louder, she learned to pick the lock.

CHAPTER 2

PROVE IT WITH WORK, NOT WORDS

*When they question your place,
let your results answer.*
Patrice Banks.

Patrice Banks was tired. Tired of being talked down to at auto repair shops, tired of mechanics assuming she didn't understand her own car, tired of being overcharged because she was a woman.

She had two choices: keep complaining or learn to fix cars herself. She chose the wrench.

Patrice walked into a mechanic class as the only woman in a room full of teenage boys. She worked in garages where people questioned why she was there. She studied until she earned her ASE certification. Then she opened Girls Auto Clinic—a shop by women, for women, teaching women they didn't need to be intimidated by their own vehicles.

She wrote a bestselling book, built a franchise, and created a movement. All because she refused to accept that auto repair wasn't for her.

When you're the "different" one in the room, you notice what others miss. That difference isn't a disadvantage. It's your opening.

This is how you turn being the "opposite" into opportunity.

Reader's Transition

Some people fill rooms with noise. They talk about what they are going to do, explain why they belong, and defend their right to be there. Doers skip the talking. They just do the work.

When you walk into a space where nobody expects to see you, you have two choices. You can spend your energy convincing people you belong, or you can spend it proving you belong. One is exhausting. The other is undeniable.

The truth is, when you are the opposite in the room, people watch you differently. They are waiting for you to fail, hoping you will prove their assumptions right. You cannot talk your way past that. You cannot charm through it. You cannot convince them.

The only thing that works? Results. Build proof, not arguments. Not explanations. Not defenses. Just work, consistent, excellent, undeniable work. That is how you win rooms that were not built for you.

This pattern appears across every industry. Patrice was a woman in auto shops, but being the different one reveals opportunities everywhere. In tech, it is the liberal arts major who notices user design problems engineers miss. In finance, it is the woman who sees how advisors talk down to female clients. In education, it is the first generation college student who understands barriers that traditional teachers do not see.

As you read Patrice's story, ask yourself: What do I notice because of my difference that others in my field consistently miss?

Origin

Phoenixville, Pennsylvania.

Patrice Banks grows up in a working class neighborhood. Her mother raises her alone, no father in the picture, not much money ever. Patrice is biracial, and in some spaces she is too Black while in others she is not Black enough. She learns early what it feels like to be the opposite everywhere you go.

The house is not safe. There is abuse, yelling, and fear. Home is the place you survive, not the place you rest. At sixteen, Patrice buys her first car, not for fun, but for escape. That car means freedom. It means she can leave when things get bad, that she controls something in her life, that she is not trapped. She loves that car not because it is fancy, but because it is hers.

School is her other escape. She is an honors student, smart, focused, determined to get out. She is the first person in her family to graduate high school, the first to even think about college. Lehigh University offers her a thirty-two-thousand-dollar scholarship, a full ride for materials science and engineering. She takes it, works hard, and graduates.

By her twenties, Patrice has a job at DuPont, a real job in engineering and management making six figures. She made it. She escaped poverty, broke the cycle, and proved everyone wrong who said kids from her neighborhood do not make it.

But something still does not feel right. She has imposter syndrome even with the degree, the salary, and the success. She feels like she is playing a role, like someone is going to figure out she does not really belong. And she wants her work to matter more, to help people, to make a difference beyond corporate profits.

But there is another problem, a smaller problem that grows bigger every time it happens. Her car.

Play by Play

The problem nobody sees.

Patrice is a materials science engineer. She understands systems, can read technical diagrams, and knows how things work. But when she takes her car to the mechanic, she feels stupid.

The mechanics talk down to her, use words she doesn't understand, and make her feel like she's bothering them by asking questions. They overcharge her—she knows they do, but she doesn't know enough to argue. They upsell unnecessary repairs: "You need this fixed or your engine will fail." She has no way to know if that's true. Sometimes they hit on her. Sometimes they ignore her. Sometimes they talk to her like she's a child.

Every time she needs her car fixed, she dreads it. This successful engineer with a six-figure salary feels helpless about her own car.

She thinks: There has to be a female mechanic in Philadelphia. Someone who won't treat me like this. She searches, calls around, asks friends. Nothing. Not one female mechanic in the entire Philadelphia area.

That's when it clicks. If I can't find one, I'll become one.

The pivot.

She is thirty-one years old with a great job and a stable career. People would think she is crazy. She enrolls anyway, Delaware Technical Community College, night classes in automotive technology.

She walks into class the first day as the only woman, surrounded by nineteen-year-old boys. They stare. Some laugh. Some do not take her seriously. She does not care. She came to learn.

For two years, she works her engineering job during the day and goes to mechanic school at night and on weekends whenever she can. People at DuPont think she is having a midlife crisis. "Why would an engineer learn to fix cars?" She does not explain. She just keeps going.

She graduates from automotive school in 2013. One month later, she quits DuPont and walks away from the six figure salary, the stability, and the career she worked so hard to build. Her family thinks she has lost her mind. Her friends do not understand.

But Patrice is clear. She is done playing small, done feeling helpless, done working for someone else's mission.

She has her own mission now.

Building from the bottom.

She works in Philadelphia garages for free, just to get experience, to learn the business side, to understand how shops operate. Then she takes a job at a repair shop where they pay her 600 dollars a week.

From six figures to 600 a week. Most people would call that failure. Patrice calls it investment.

While she is working at that shop, she starts teaching car care workshops for women, free classes showing women how to check their oil, change a tire, and understand what mechanics are telling them. Women show up. Lots of women. They are hungry for this knowledge, tired of feeling stupid, tired of being taken advantage of.

Patrice writes a book: *Girls Auto Clinic Glove Box Guide*. A simple manual teaching women about their cars in plain language with no jargon, just practical help. She publishes it in 2017.

That same year, she opens Girls Auto Clinic in Upper Darby, Pennsylvania. Not just a repair shop—a completely different model.

Breakthrough

The shop that changes everything.

Girls Auto Clinic has transparent pricing, no games, no up-selling, just honest service. It has free monthly workshops where women can learn car care in a safe space. It has a kids' area so moms can bring their children and not worry.

And here is the part that made everyone laugh: it has Clutch Beauty Bar, a nail salon and beauty bar attached to the repair shop. The idea came from seeing a Jiffy Lube next to a nail salon. Patrice thought, *"Why not combine them?"* Women can get a manicure while their car gets fixed.

The auto industry mocked her. "A beauty salon in a repair shop? That is ridiculous." "Women do not want to learn about cars." "This will never work." Patrice did not argue. She just opened the doors.

Women showed up in waves. They came because they felt safe, because they were treated with respect, because they could ask questions without being dismissed. They came because the pricing was honest, because the mechanics explained things clearly, because they left understanding their car instead of feeling confused.

Within one year, Patrice hired five female mechanics, all women who contacted her wanting to enter the profession, women who had been told they did not belong in auto shops. She created apprenticeships for women studying to become technicians, training the next generation. She started the #sheCANic movement, promoting female inclusion in the automotive industry.

By 2018, women made up 75 percent of her clientele, not because she only served women, but because she created a space where women felt valued.

The recognition.

The media noticed: TIME, Forbes, Glamour, NPR, The Washington Post, Oprah Magazine. Partnerships followed with the Renewable Fuels Association and other organizations wanting to support her mission.

In 2019, Fox considered a TV pilot based on her story called Patty's Auto. They passed on it, but the fact that they considered it at all proved how far she had come.

In 2025, Patrice Banks was inducted into the African American Automotive Association Hall of Fame.

From the only woman in her mechanic class to the Hall of Fame. From feeling helpless at auto shops to building the auto shop she wished existed. From 600 dollars a week to running a thriving business that changed an industry.

That is not luck. That is what happens when you prove it with work instead of words.

Power Moves

1. Use your "opposite" status to see what others miss

When you're the different one in the room, you notice things others don't—the gaps, the problems, the people being ignored. Patrice was a woman in auto shops, and she felt the dismissal, the overcharging, the intimidation. She lived the problem. Male shop owners didn't see it because they weren't experiencing it.

Your difference is your advantage. It gives you a lens others don't have. Use it. What do you see that others miss? What problem do you understand because you've lived it? That's your opportunity.

2. Build proof, not arguments

Patrice could have spent years arguing that women deserve respect in auto shops. She could have written articles, given speeches, and demanded change. Instead, she built a shop that worked. She fixed cars, taught classes, and published a book. Her business proved her point better than any argument ever could.

When you're the underdog, nobody gives you credit for potential. They only care about proof. Did you do the thing? Did it work? Can you do it again? Stop explaining. Start building.

3. Show up consistently when the doubt is loudest

Patrice walked into mechanic class as the only woman surrounded by teenage boys. She worked in garages where people questioned why she was there. She opened a shop while people said it would fail. The doubt never stopped. She just kept showing up—every class, every shift, every workshop, every customer.

Consistency beats doubt. Not immediately, but eventually. When you show up over and over doing excellent work, people stop questioning—not because you convinced them, but because you proved them wrong.

4. Let your work do the talking

Patrice did not spend energy defending her right to be in the auto industry. She spent it fixing cars, teaching women, and building a business. Her work spoke louder than any defense ever could.

When you are the opposite, the temptation is to explain yourself, to justify your presence, to convince people you belong. Resist that. Save your energy for the work. Because at the end of the day, results are the only currency that matters. People can ignore your words. They cannot ignore your results.

Mind Trap

The Belonging Mind Trap: "I don't really deserve to be here"

Here is what happens even after you start winning, even after you have the credentials, even after you prove yourself. There is a voice in your head that says, "You got lucky. You are a fraud. They are going to figure out you do not really belong here."

That is imposter syndrome. And it does not care about your accomplishments. It attacks everyone, especially underdogs.

Patrice felt it. She had a degree from Lehigh, twelve years at DuPont, and a six figure salary. And she still felt like an imposter.

Why does this happen? Because when you are the opposite in a space, you internalize all the doubt directed at you, all the questions, all the skepticism. Your brain hears "women do not belong in auto shops" or "people from your background do not become engineers" so many times that it starts believing it. Even when you succeed, your brain says, "That was luck. A fluke. It will not happen again."

And the cruel part is the higher you climb, the louder the voice gets. Because now the stakes are higher, now more people are watching, now there is more to lose. So the voice says, "Any day now, they will see you are not good enough. They will realize you do not belong. They will send you back where you came from."

Here is the truth: that voice is lying. It is not based on facts. It is based on fear, fear of being exposed, fear of failing, fear of confirming other people's biases. But the facts say something different. You did earn your place. You did do the work. You are good enough.

The voice will not disappear. Even successful people hear it. The difference is they do not let it stop them.

The fix is action, not confidence. You do not have to feel like you belong to act like you belong. You do not have to feel confident to be good at what you do. You just have to keep moving, keep building, keep showing up.

Every time you deliver results, the voice gets a little quieter, not silent, but quieter. Every time you prove you can do it again, the doubt fades a little more.

Patrice probably still hears the voice sometimes: "Did I make the right choice? Can I really run this business? What if it fails?" But she does not let it stop her. She just keeps fixing cars, teaching women, and showing up. Because competence comes from doing, not from feeling. And the more you do, the more proof you build, against the doubters outside and against the doubt inside.

So when the voice says "you do not belong here," you do not have to argue with it. Just do the work. Let your results be the answer.

Modern Reflection

The old rule was simple: fit in or get out. If you were the opposite in a space, you had to work twice as hard for half the credit, prove yourself over and over, and even then people questioned your place. That rule still exists in many spaces. But something has changed.

Now you can build your own spaces.

Patrice could not find a female mechanic in Philadelphia, so she became one and then built a whole business model around serving women. She did not wait for the auto industry to change. She just built the alternative.

That is the move for 2025 and beyond. When traditional spaces will not make room for you, build your own room. The tools make it easier now. Want to teach but schools will not hire you? Build an online course. Want to create but galleries will not show you? Build a following on Instagram. Want to write but publishers will not pick you? Start a Substack. Want to speak but conferences will not book you? Start a podcast.

You do not need permission anymore. You need WiFi and work ethic.

Patrice built Girls Auto Clinic in 2017. Imagine if she had TikTok, she could have taught car care to millions before ever opening a physical shop.

Being the opposite is actually an advantage now because you see gaps others do not, understand problems others miss, and can serve communities others ignore. And in the age of the internet, those communities can find you. Even if you are the only one like you in your city, you can build an audience of thousands who relate to you.

The woman who teaches plus size women how to dress. The man who teaches stay at home dads how to meal prep. The person who teaches first generation college students how to navigate campus. Niches are not weaknesses anymore. They are strengths. Because the riches are in the niches, as they say.

Here is what has not changed: you still have to build proof. You still have to show up consistently. You still have to do excellent work. Being the opposite gets people's attention, but only results keep their trust.

The difference now is you can build proof publicly. Document your journey. Share what you are learning. Let people watch you grow. Patrice built in private for years before going public. You can build in public from day one.

Every workshop you teach, every customer you serve, every problem you solve, share it. Not to brag, but to build credibility, to show you are doing the work. Because when you are the opposite in a space, people want to see proof before they believe you.

So give them proof. Consistently. Publicly. Undeniably. Then watch what happens when your work speaks louder than their doubts.

Patrice Banks saw a problem others missed because she lived it. She used her outsider status as a lens, then built proof that silenced every doubt.

That is powerful. But there is something even more powerful: when your mission is not just about proving yourself but about changing the lives of everyone who comes after you.

Patrice built a business that taught women they did not need to be intimidated by mechanics. Over a century earlier, another woman built something bigger, an economic movement that lifted thousands of families out of poverty.

She started with less than Issa. Less than Patrice. Less than almost anyone. She started with 1 dollar and 50 cents and a washtub. And she changed American history.

CHAPTER 3

BUILD YOUR OWN DOOR WHEN THEY LOCK YOU OUT

> *When no one gives you a chance, make your own chance.*
> **Madam C.J. Walker.**

Sarah Breedlove was born to formerly enslaved parents in a Louisiana cotton field. She was orphaned at seven, married at fourteen, and widowed at twenty, a single mother scrubbing other people's clothes to survive.

She could not read. She had 1 dollar and 50 cents to her name. By every measure, she should have stayed invisible.

Instead, she became Madam C. J. Walker, the first female self-made millionaire in American history. She did not guess what Black women needed. She knew. She felt their pain because it was her pain too, hair loss, scalp conditions, and a beauty industry that ignored them completely.

So she mixed her first batch of hair care formula in a washtub, tested it on herself, improved it, and sold it door to door. Then she built something bigger, a network of thousands of sales agents, Black women who became financially independent by selling her products. Women who supported families, sent children to college, and bought homes.

Walker did not just build a business. She built an economic movement.

When your mission is bigger than your fear, nothing can stop you.

This is how you start with a problem you know in your bones and turn it into legacy.

Reader's Transition

The world is full of locked doors. Some people spend their whole lives knocking, waiting, and hoping someone will let them in. While they wait, they watch others walk through. They make excuses, blame the system, and grow bitter.

Smart underdogs don't wait. They build their own door. You cannot sit around hoping things will change. You must change them yourself.

Mission-driven courage drives change in all industries. Walker built a beauty empire, but the same principle applies everywhere. In tech, it's building accessibility features because you have a disabled family member. In healthcare, it's opening a clinic in the underserved area where you grew up. In education, it's creating scholarships for students who face the barriers you once faced.

As you read Walker's story, ask yourself: What problem do I understand so deeply—from lived experience— that solving it matters more than the risk of trying?

Origin

Late 1800s. Louisiana.

Sarah Breedlove was born on a cotton farm. Her parents were slaves. By age seven, both of her parents passed, and she was alone. She married at fourteen and by twenty, her husband was dead too, and she had a baby girl to feed with no money and no help.

Life got harder. Her hair started falling out, and the cheap products she used burned her scalp. Every day she felt uglier, smaller, more invisible. The world told her: Stay down. This is where you belong.

She made a different choice.

Play by Play

The beginning.

Sarah did not have money for fancy hair treatments, so she made her own. She mixed oils and herbs in a washtub, tried different recipes, and tested them on herself. When her hair grew back, something clicked: other women have this same problem. I can help them.

She had 1 dollar and 25 cents in her pocket. That is it. No store, no factory, no business training. But she had something better, she knew the problem from the inside. She lived it. She understood the pain.

She started walking door to door, selling her hair treatment to Black women one at a time. She did not just sell bottles. She sold hope. She told women, "*You are beautiful.*" You deserve to feel proud. The women listened. They bought, and they told their friends.

In 1906, she married Charles Joseph Walker. She took his name and made it famous. She became Madam C. J. Walker.

Breakthrough

The system that changed everything.

Here is what made Walker different: she did not just build a company. She built a system. She trained other women to sell her products, women called "Walker Agents" who went door to door in their own towns, made their own money, and built their own businesses.

In 1910, most Black women had no way to earn money. They worked in white people's homes or in fields with no power and no choices. Walker changed that. Her agents did not work for her, they worked with her. When Walker made money, they made money. When they won, she won.

Thousands of women joined. They earned, they saved, they bought homes, and they sent their kids to school. Walker did not keep the money for herself. She gave to schools, funded groups fighting racism, and helped other Black people start businesses.

By 1919, when she died, she was a millionaire, one of the first American women to earn that much money herself, not from marriage or family wealth, but from her own hands.

From 1 dollar and 25 cents to a million dollars. From invisible to unstoppable.

Power Moves

1. Start with the problem you know best

Walker didn't guess what women needed. She knew. She felt their pain because it was her pain too. Your power comes from problems you understand deeply. What keeps you up at night? What makes you angry? What do you wish existed? That's where you start.

2. Begin small but begin now

Walker didn't wait for a factory or investors. She mixed her first batch in a washtub. Sara Blakely cut the feet off her pantyhose before starting Spanx. You don't need everything to start—you need something. One customer, one product, one step.

Perfect is the enemy of done. Start messy. Start small. Just start.

3. Build others up as you rise

Walker became powerful because she made others powerful. Her agents succeeded when she succeeded. Their families won when they won. Real power isn't hoarding—it's sharing. When you lift others, they lift you higher.

4. Make your mission bigger than your fear

Walker had every reason to quit. She was poor, Black, a woman, a widow. The whole world was against her. But her why was bigger. She wanted women to feel beautiful, feel proud, feel free.

When your why is bigger than your fear, nothing can stop you.

Mind Trap

Don't mistake busy for building: "I have to stay busy."

Here is what happens when people finally decide to move. They get excited, see all the possibilities, and want to do everything at once. So they start ten projects, sign up for five courses, begin three businesses, and join four groups. They feel productive and busy, and they tell everyone they are hustling.

But six months later, nothing is finished. Nothing is working. They are exhausted and confused.

Why does this happen? Because starting feels like progress. It gives you a rush. Your brain releases dopamine when you begin something new, and it feels good to imagine success. But finishing, finishing is hard. Finishing is boring. Finishing means doing the same thing over and over until it works. Your brain does not reward that the same way.

So people become addicted to starting. They jump from idea to idea, chase the feeling of newness, and confuse motion with movement.

Here is the truth: one finished door is worth more than ten half built ones.

Walker did not start a haircare line and a restaurant and a clothing brand. She picked one problem, solved it completely, and made it work before moving on. That focus is what made her a millionaire.

The fix is simple but not easy: pick one door, the one that matters most, the one you understand best, the one that solves a real problem. Build it strong. Build it all the way. Make it work. Then, and only then, build another.

Starting ten things does not build momentum. It burns it. Your power comes from depth, not width. From finishing, not starting.

Choose your door. Build it right. Open it wide. Everything else can wait.

Modern Reflection

The old rules are broken. For years, the path was simple: good grades, college degree, steady job, climb the ladder. That formula is dead.

In 2020, twenty-two million people lost their jobs. By 2024, companies stopped hiring. AI is replacing thirty percent of jobs by 2030, customer service, data entry, basic office work. Gone. But here is the good news: this levels the field.

Companies now care about what you can do, not where you went to school. The tools that used to cost millions are now free. Anyone can learn AI, build online, and prove their worth. The door that was closed? You do not need it anymore.

And here is what people miss: being an underdog is an advantage. When no one believes in you, you are free. No reputation to protect, no pressure to play it safe. You can try things others will not, move faster than they can, and break rules they are afraid to touch.

Madam C. J. Walker proved this over one hundred years ago. Born a slave, died a millionaire, not because she got lucky, but because she built her own door.

The blueprint still works. The game has changed, but the moves stay the same. When they lock you out, build your own way in. Your background does not matter. Your resources do not matter. Your connections do not matter.

What matters is this: do you see the problem? Will you start the solution? Will you take the first step?

Because one small act of courage can become an empire. One door you build can open a thousand more. The world will not make space for you. So stop asking. Start creating.

Madam C. J. Walker built an empire by starting with the problem she knew best, testing relentlessly, and lifting others as she rose. Her mission was bigger than her fear, and that mission changed thousands of lives.

But here is something remarkable: Walker did not invent her business model alone. She learned it from a woman named Annie Turnbo Malone. Walker worked for Malone as a sales agent before starting her own company. She saw Malone's system up close, watched how it worked, and learned from it. Then she built her own version.

Some people saw this as betrayal. But Malone saw it differently. She saw it as proof, proof that her system worked, proof that it was teachable, proof that when you document your methods instead of hoarding your secrets, you create something that multiplies beyond you.

Walker built an empire. Malone built the blueprint for building empires.

This is what happens when you systematize success.

PART TWO
PROOF IN MOTION

Momentum is louder than talk. Build proof — even when no one's watching.

The hardest part of any journey isn't starting.

It's staying.

The early days are fueled by adrenaline, new ideas, new energy, the thrill of finally beginning. But once the excitement fades and the work becomes routine, self-doubt creeps in. The applause dies down. The proof is still invisible. That is the moment where most people quit.

Not because they failed, but because they could not see progress yet.

Part II is about what happens after the first leap, when you are building quietly, refining your craft, and doing the work that does not always get celebrated. It is about how to turn early momentum into lasting credibility.

Because results do not appear all at once. They stack slowly, often in silence. Every draft you finish, every small project completed, every relationship strengthened, that is proof in motion. It might not trend, but it compounds. It earns trust. It builds reputation. And eventually, it opens doors you once had to build yourself.

In these chapters, you will see how underdogs became unstoppable not through instant breakthroughs, but through patient consistency. They built trust before titles. They mastered follow through before recognition. They learned that being underestimated is temporary, but being consistent is permanent.

Proof doesn't come from talking about what you'll do next.

It comes from *doing it again*.

And that's your next challenge: Keep showing up.

Keep stacking the wins that no one else can see yet.

Because sooner or later, those quiet repetitions become undeniable.

Start small. Stay steady. Build proof.

Your momentum is your message.

CHAPTER 4

TEACH WHAT YOU KNOW, MULTIPLY WHAT YOU BUILD

*When you teach others to build,
your legacy builds itself.*
Annie Turnbo Malone.

Most people know Madam C.J. Walker's name. Fewer know Annie Turnbo Malone—even though Walker learned the hair care business working for her.

But here's what makes Annie's story remarkable: while Walker built an empire, Annie built the blueprint for building empires. She didn't just create successful products. She created a system for success that 75,000 women could replicate.

Annie wrote everything down—formulas, techniques, training manuals, sales scripts, business processes. She turned her personal knowledge into transferable power. Her agents didn't just sell products, they learned to run businesses. They became financially independent. They built wealth in their communities.

Annie avoided the spotlight. No big speeches, no celebrity, just quiet, methodical documentation of what worked.

And that documentation created something that outlasted fame: a system that multiplied success across thousands of lives.

This is how you scale—not by keeping secrets, but by creating systems others can follow.

Reader's Transition

Most people think knowledge is power when you keep it. They guard their secrets, protect their methods, and think: "If I teach others what I know, they'll compete with me." That's scarcity thinking, and scarcity thinking keeps you small.

Smart underdogs know better. They understand that knowledge is power when it moves. When you teach one person, you double your impact. When you teach ten, you multiply it. When you build a system that teaches thousands, you create something that outlives you.

You don't just build success for yourself. You build systems that teach others to build too. Because when you teach others to climb, you don't slow down. You strengthen your foundation.

Documentation creates scale across every industry. Annie systematized beauty education, but the principle applies everywhere. In tech, it's writing code documentation so other developers can contribute. In healthcare, it's creating clinical protocols any provider on your team can follow. In consulting, it's building frameworks that clients can use after your engagement ends.

As you read Annie's story, ask yourself: What do I do well that I could document clearly enough for someone else to replicate my results?

Origin

Late 1800s. Metropolis, Illinois.

Annie Turnbo is born the tenth of eleven children. Her parents were slaves before freedom came. By the time she's young, both parents are dead. Gone. An older sister takes her in and raises her in Peoria, Illinois. They have almost nothing.

Annie's frequent illness forces her to leave high school early. No diploma, no formal education, just a girl who spends too much time in bed, staring at the ceiling, wondering if life will always be this hard.

But she notices something during those long, sick days. Her hair. Her sister's hair. Her friends' hair. It's breaking, falling out, damaged. The products available to Black women are terrible—goose fat, heavy oils, bacon grease, harsh chemicals that burn more than they help.

Annie wonders if there's a better way.

While other people complain, Annie studies. She reads everything she can about chemistry, about hair, about scalp health. She mixes ingredients in her sister's kitchen, tests them on herself, adjusts, and tries again. Most people would have given up. No money, no education, no lab. Just a sick girl in a kitchen with big ideas.

Annie keeps going.

Play by Play

Building something that works.

By 1900, Annie has something that works, a formula called "Wonderful Hair Grower." It is safe, it is effective, and it makes hair healthier instead of destroying it. But she has a problem. She is a Black woman with no money, no store, no distribution system, making products in the back of a tiny building and mixing batches by hand.

The world is not going to make room for her, so she makes her own room. She buys a horse and buggy, loads up her products, and starts going door to door, not just selling, but teaching, demonstrating, showing women what healthy hair can look like. Listening to their pain, understanding their shame, giving them hope. One woman at a time, one door at a time, one town at a time.

The sales come slowly, but they come. Women try the products, their hair grows back and gets healthier and stronger, and they tell their friends. Word spreads not through ads but through results.

The system emerges.

By 1902, Annie moves to St. Louis and starts the Poro Company. The name comes from a West African term meaning "devotional society." This is not just business. It is mission.

But here is where Annie does something different, something most people would never think to do. She starts teaching other women her methods, not just how to sell her products, but how to run a business, how to talk to customers, how to manage money, how to present themselves, how to lead.

One woman asks, "How did you do this?" Annie does not say, "That is my secret." She says, "Let me show you." Then another woman asks, so Annie shows her too. Then ten women, then a hundred.

At some point, she realizes, I need a system. A structure. A place to teach properly. In 1918 she opens Poro College.

Breakthrough

Building the institution.

Poro College is not just a beauty school. It is a business academy. A movement. Women learn chemistry, sales, accounting, presentation skills, and self-confidence. This is decades before business schools admit women, decades before Black women have access to higher education, decades before anyone thinks to teach entrepreneurship to people the world wrote off.

Annie does not wait for permission. She builds the institution that should exist.

At its peak, Poro College occupies a full city block in St. Louis, classrooms, a manufacturing plant, an auditorium, a bakery, a dining hall, an ice cream parlor, a rooftop garden. It employs over two hundred people and trains thousands of "Poro Agents" across the country and around the world.

Annie becomes one of the first Black women millionaires in America, not by keeping her secrets, but by sharing them. Her students do not just learn. They build. They open their own territories, hire their own teams, and train their own students.

The proof.

Here's the proof that Annie's system worked: One of her students was Madam C.J. Walker. Walker worked as a Poro agent, learned Annie's methods, saw the business model up close, and understood how teaching and systems could multiply success. Then Walker went on to build her own empire, training thousands more women using the same principle: teach others to build.

Annie didn't lose by teaching Walker. She multiplied. Walker's success proved Annie's model worked everywhere, not just in one place. That's the power of teaching what you know. One teacher creates thousands of builders, and those builders create thousands more.

The hard years.

But Annie's journey wasn't easy, even after success came. A painful divorce cost her $200,000—her ex-husband claimed he built the business, not her, and demanded half. The court battle drained her. The Great Depression hit in 1929, and her fortune crumbled. She had to move the business to Chicago to restart. Lawsuits piled up from former employees, financial problems grew, and by 1951, the government seized the company for unpaid taxes.

Annie died in 1957—not rich, not famous, mostly forgotten. For decades, Walker got all the credit while Annie's name faded.

But here's what they couldn't take from her: the thousands of women she taught, the businesses they built, the lives they changed, the system she created that shaped an entire industry.

From an orphaned girl too sick to finish school to a millionaire who built builders. From a kitchen mixing bowl to a full-city-block college. From invisible to undeniable. Not by keeping secrets, but by giving them away.

That's not just business. That's blueprint.

Power Moves

1. Document what you do well

Annie did not just keep her formulas in her head. She wrote them down, created training manuals, and built processes others could follow. That is what made her business scalable, she was not the only one who could make it work. Thousands could make it work.

When you document your methods, you create your future blueprint. You turn personal knowledge into shared power. What do you do well that you could write down? Not perfectly, just clearly enough that someone else could follow it.

2. Create systems, not secrets

Most people think: "If I teach my secrets, people will steal them." Annie thought: "If I teach my methods, they'll prove my system works everywhere." She was right. Her students' success validated her approach, made her model stronger, and extended her reach to places she'd never go herself.

Systems multiply. Secrets die with you.

3. Lead quietly through results

Annie avoided the spotlight. She didn't give big speeches, didn't chase fame, didn't build a personal brand. She just showed up every day, did the work, delivered results, and built systems. Her students followed her not because she demanded it, but because she earned it.

In a world full of noise, the person who stays steady stands out. Quiet consistency outlasts loud ambition every time. Your calm is your advantage.

4. Build builders, not fans

Anyone can inspire, tell a good story, share some quotes, get people excited. But inspiration without education is just entertainment. Annie did not want fans. She wanted students who could build their own empires. She gave them skills that turned confidence into competence, knowledge that turned effort into income.

She was not building an audience. She was building entrepreneurs. That is the difference between a movement that fades and a legacy that lasts.

Mind Trap

The Scarcity Mind Trap: "If I teach them, they'll replace me"

Here is what happens when people get good at something. They start protecting it, guarding it, keeping it close. They think, "This knowledge is my advantage. If I share it, I lose my edge." So they stay quiet. They do not teach. They do not document. They hold everything inside.

And ten years later, they are still doing everything themselves, still maxed out, still stuck at the same level.

Why does this happen? Because your brain is wired for scarcity. For thousands of years, resources were limited, food, shelter, safety. If you shared, you had less. That instinct made sense then. It does not make sense now.

Knowledge is not food. Teaching someone does not leave you with less knowledge. It leaves you with an ally, a partner, a multiplier. But your brain does not know that. It still screams, "Do not share. You will lose your advantage."

Here is the truth: the person who teaches grows faster than the person who hoards. When you teach, you understand your own methods deeper. You see gaps you missed. You refine your thinking. You get better by explaining.

And the person you teach, they do not replace you. They extend you. They reach customers you would never reach. They improve on your ideas. They prove your system works.

Annie Malone taught thousands, including Madam C. J. Walker, who became more famous than Annie ever was.

Did that hurt Annie? No. It proved her model worked. It validated her approach. It multiplied her impact.

The fix is simple but not easy: stop thinking about knowledge as property. Start thinking about it as seed. When you plant a seed, you do not have less. You have more. The seed grows into a tree. The tree makes more seeds. Those seeds become a forest.

That is what teaching does. One person taught becomes ten people building. Ten people become a hundred. A hundred become a movement. But only if you are willing to plant the first seed.

The question is not, "What if they steal my knowledge?" The question is, "What if my knowledge dies with me?" Teach. Document. Share. Build systems that outlive you. That is not weakness. That is legacy.

Modern Reflection

The old model of success was, learn a skill, guard it closely, use it to climb. That model is dead.

We live in the creator economy now. The people winning are not the ones hoarding knowledge, they are the ones teaching it. Online courses, YouTube tutorials, newsletters, podcasts, cohort programs. People are building million dollar businesses by teaching what they know.

And AI makes knowledge hoarding pointless. Any information can be found in seconds. The skill is not knowing facts anymore, it is knowing how to apply them, how to think, how to build. You cannot Google wisdom. You cannot AI generate experience. That only comes from people who have done the work and are willing to teach it.

Here is what that means for you: the person who documents their process wins. The person who teaches their methods builds faster. The person who creates systems scales further.

Companies do not just want employees anymore, they want people who can train teams, build processes, and turn one success into repeatable results. Freelancers who teach their craft charge more than freelancers who just do the work. Entrepreneurs who build systems exit bigger than entrepreneurs who are the system.

Building in public is not just trendy. It is strategic. When you share what you are learning, you attract allies, people who think like you, people who want to build with you, people who become customers, partners, investors, or champions.

Annie built Poro College in 1918. Imagine what she could have done with the internet. You have tools she never dreamed of, platforms that can reach millions, software that can automate teaching, communities that can form instantly. The barrier is not access anymore. It is courage. The courage to share what you know before you feel expert enough.

Here is the move: stop waiting to be perfect. Start teaching what you are learning right now. Document your process. Share your experiments. Show your work. Invite others to build with you.

Because the person who teaches becomes the leader. The person who shares becomes the center. The person who builds systems becomes the architect. And architects build things that last.

Annie Turnbo Malone showed us the power of systems. When you document what works, create repeatable processes, and teach others to follow them, you build something that scales far beyond your individual effort.

Her seventy-five thousand agents proved it: systems multiply. Secrets die with you.

But here is the question: what happens when the system rejects you? What do you do when you follow the rules, show up consistently, work hard, and the corporate system keeps spitting you out?

Annie built a system that welcomed people. But not every system is built that way.

Charis Jones tried to succeed inside corporate America. She worked hard, brought creativity, and delivered results. And got fired. Three times.

She could have believed the system's verdict, "You do not fit." Instead, she asked, "What is the pattern here?" That question changed everything.

CHAPTER 5

TURN REJECTION INTO REDIRECTION

*Don't wait for permission to fit.
Build your own space instead.*
Charis Jones.

Charis Jones got fired. Then she got fired again. Then she got fired a third time.

Most people would take it personally, question their worth, and wonder what's wrong with them. Charis asked a different question: "What's the pattern?"

The pattern wasn't "I'm bad at my job." The pattern was "Corporate structures don't fit creative, bold people who think differently." That wasn't defeat. That was data.

So she stopped trying to fit into systems that rejected her. She built her own. From her kitchen, while caring for twin babies, Charis launched Sassy Jones—a jewelry business that started with trade shows and pivoted to livestream shopping when the trade show model stopped working.

She sold her car, maxed out credit cards, and built a pop-up studio in her home. Her "Sparkle Parties" became must-watch events where thousands of viewers tuned in weekly—not just for jewelry, but for community.

Getting fired three times wasn't failure. It was preparation for building something no corporation could contain.

This is how you read rejection as research—and use it to build better.

Reader's Transition

Some people get fired once and freeze. They spiral, doubt, and wonder what's wrong with them. Then there are people who get fired three times and launch. They don't see rejection as proof they're broken. They see it as proof they're in the wrong place.

This is the move for people who've been told they don't fit, who've been let go, passed over, or rejected repeatedly. You have two choices when the door closes: stare at it or build a new one. Most people stare. They mourn what they lost, wish things were different, and wait for someone to let them back in.

Smart underdogs build. They take what's left, use it to create what's next, and turn the firing into fuel. Because rejection isn't failure. It's redirection. It's information about where you don't belong so you can find where you do.

Charis Jones got fired from three Fortune 500 jobs. She could've given up, could've believed she wasn't good enough. Instead, she sold her Mercedes, bought jewelry inventory, and started selling from her car trunk. Today, Sassy Jones is a multimillion-dollar brand featured in Forbes and on the Inc. 5000 list, built entirely without investors—not despite the firings, but because of them.

Because sometimes rock bottom isn't the end. It's the launch pad.

Rejection-as-data reveals patterns across every industry. Charis got fired from corporate three times, but the principle applies everywhere. In tech, it's VCs all saying "too niche"—meaning you've found an underserved market. In creative fields, it's publishers rejecting your manuscript 50 times, all citing "no market"—so you self-publish and prove them wrong. In trades, it's companies that won't hire you because of discrimination—so you start your own.

As you read Charis's story, ask yourself: What pattern emerges when I look at my rejections not as personal failures but as data about misalignment?

Origin

October 31, 1982. United States.

Charis Jones is born to a teenage mother who can't raise her. Her grandparents step in and become her parents. Her grandmother becomes her world.

Charis watches her grandmother—the way she dresses, the elegant handbags, the poised style, the strength she carries even when things are hard. At five years old, Charis steals her grandmother's handbags, runs off with them, plays dress-up, and falls in love with accessories. Her grandmother doesn't get mad. She sees the spark, the creativity, the girl who wants to create beauty.

Growing up, Charis carries something heavy: abandonment issues. Her mother wasn't there, and that hurt stays.

But her grandmother shows her something else—you can survive anything, keep your family together, and stay elegant even when life isn't. Charis learns resilience by watching, learns style by copying, and learns that you don't need perfect circumstances to be powerful.

Her grandmother tells her: "You can conquer anything that you set your mind to." Charis believes her.

Hampton University. Early 2000s.

Charis studies at Hampton, learning about marketplace differentiation, building customer relationships, and business fundamentals. She's smart, capable, and ready to take on the corporate world. After graduation, she lands jobs in sales and marketing at Fortune 500 companies—good money, the kind of positions people chase.

She should be happy. She should feel like she made it. But she doesn't fit.

Play by Play

The corporate rejection pattern.

Job one: sales and marketing at a Fortune 500 company in Hampton, Virginia. Charis works hard, shows up, tries to follow the rules and be the employee they want. It does not work. They let her go. She is confused and hurt. She thinks, Maybe I made a mistake. I will do better next time.

Job two: another Fortune 500 company, another sales and marketing role with a financial services background. She tries harder this time, adjusts, fits in better, and does everything right. They fire her anyway. Now she is scared. Two firings. What is wrong with me? Am I not good enough?

Job three: one more corporate job, high paying and prestigious in financial services. She is desperate to make this one work; needs to prove she belongs here. But the same thing happens, her creativity does not fit their structure, her energy does not match their culture, her ideas are too different. They fire her.

Three times. Three different companies. Same result. Most people would break here, would believe the message: You are not good enough. You do not belong. Give up. Charis feels inadequate and questions everything about herself.

But then something shifts. She realizes, it is not that I am wrong. It is that these places are wrong for me. Corporate structures do not fit creative people who think differently, who challenge norms, who want to build something new. The firings were not proof she was broken. They were proof she needed a different path.

The pivot moment.

June 2013, Hampton, Virginia. Charis is driving to her corporate job again, still trying to fit in, still feeling like she doesn't belong. The radio is on. A commercial plays: Trade show coming to town. Vendors wanted.

Something clicks. What if I could sell the accessories I love? What if I didn't need someone else's permission to do work that matters?

The idea won't leave her alone. She thinks about her grandmother—the handbags, the style, the confidence beautiful accessories can give a woman. She thinks about herself—always feeling like she doesn't fit, always getting pushed out. What if I built my own space? What if I made my own rules?

She decides: I'm starting a business. Sassy Jones. Sassy for the confidence she wants to give women, the unapologetic style, the audacity. Jones because it's hers.

She doesn't have investor money, doesn't have a business plan, doesn't have experience running a company. But she has a vision. And she has jewelry. That's enough to start.

The trunk years: June 2013 to 2015.

Charis launches Sassy Jones as a side business while keeping her day job and working on the jewelry business nights and weekends. She designs handcrafted jewelry—bold pieces, colorful statement necklaces, earrings, bracelets made in limited quantities. She sells her accessories from her car trunk, driving to different locations, setting up, showing women her jewelry, and making sales one piece at a time.

It's slow and hard. Some days she barely sells anything. But she keeps going because this is hers—no one can fire her from her own business. She starts attending trade shows across the country, lugging inventory, setting up booths, and pitching to customers face to face. The business grows slowly, but it grows.

The all-in moment.

Charis needs more inventory, needs to pay trade show entry fees, needs capital to grow. She doesn't have investors, doesn't have a line of credit, and banks won't give her a loan. She looks at her Mercedes—the one nice thing she owns, the symbol that she "made it" in corporate America. She sells it, takes the money, buys jewelry inventory, and pays for trade show fees.

She's all in now—no backup plan, no safety net. She also maxes out her credit cards, funding the business however she can. When she tries to lease a small office space, they deny her because her credit is wrecked. It stings, but it also fuels her. This setback is temporary. I'll build this business until I can't be denied anymore.

The crisis and the pivot.

September 2015: Charis gives birth to twin boys. Now she's not just an entrepreneur but a mother of two infants at the same time. The trade show circuit becomes impossible—she can't travel across the country with five month-old twins, can't leave them, can't do both. She's exhausted physically, financially, and emotionally.

Around the same time, her grandfather passes away. She watches her grandmother cope with the loss—it's heart-wrenching, but her grandmother stays strong, keeps going, and shows Charis what resilience looks like.

Most people would quit here. The business was barely working before, and now with two babies and grief? Impossible. But Charis doesn't quit. She pivots.

Breakthrough

The kitchen that changed everything: June 2016.

Charis is stuck at home with her twin boys, five months old and barely sleeping. The business is dying because she cannot travel to trade shows anymore. She thinks, "What if I bring the trade show to the customers?"

She builds a pop up shop in her kitchen, sets up her jewelry, styles it, and makes it look beautiful. She grabs her phone and opens Facebook. She goes live.

"Hey everyone. Welcome to The Sparkle Party."

She shows her jewelry, talks about each piece, and shares the stories behind them. Her personality shines through the screen. She is nervous, will anyone even watch? Thirteen people tune in. She makes 600 dollars in sales in one hour from her kitchen while her twins sleep upstairs.

She thinks, *"This could work."*

She does it again the next week, more viewers, more sales. Then again and again. The Sparkle Parties become weekly events, and she trademarks the name The Sparkle Party®. Customers start waiting for them, tuning in live, buying immediately, commenting, and engaging. Charis is not just selling jewelry anymore, she is building community, connection, and a space where women feel seen.

The business grows fast. By the end of 2016, she is making more money from livestreams than she ever made from trade shows.

Scaling up: 2017-2019.

The Sparkle Parties keep growing. Charis hires her husband, Keon Jones, as president of Sassy Jones—now it's a family business. She designs new jewelry lines and launches them on livestreams that sell out. She reinvests every dollar back into inventory, better equipment, and the business. No investors, no loans—just cash flow and discipline.

The company operates on American Express cards that they pay off in full every month, never carrying debt, never overextending. Sales climb—hundreds of thousands, then millions. She keeps hosting Sparkle Parties every week, showing up and building relationships with her customers.

During this time, another challenge surfaces when she hires her mother to work at Sassy Jones and old wounds resurface—unresolved abandonment issues. Her mother quits abruptly, triggering Charis. But this time, she chooses healing. She realizes her creative and emotional well-being are suffering and needs to forgive her mother for herself. They reconcile in a story of redemption, growing closer. Charis learns: You can build a business and heal yourself at the same time. Sometimes you have to.

The pandemic advantage: 2020.

The world shuts down. Businesses collapse. People panic. But Sassy Jones thrives. Why? Because Charis already built her business for digital, for connection, for community. While other businesses scramble to figure out how to sell online, Sassy Jones is already there—has been there for four years.

The Sparkle Parties become even more popular with women stuck at home, isolated, and craving connection. Charis gives them that every week—showing up, engaging, making them feel seen. Sales triple to $1.5 million per month.

Forbes notices and names Sassy Jones one of "25 small business standouts that have thrived during the pandemic." Charis Jones—the woman who got fired three times, who sold her car to start a jewelry business— featured in Forbes.

Recognition and expansion: 2022-2025.

Sassy Jones makes the Inc. 5000 list as one of the fastest-growing private companies in America. The business that started in a car trunk is now a multimillion-dollar brand—still bootstrapped, still cash-run, still no investors, still no debt. Just steady growth, community, and consistency.

Sassy Jones celebrates its 12th year in business in 2025. Charis is still CEO, still chief designer, still hosting Sparkle Parties every week. She launches the Sassy Jones Foundation, building girls' dormitories in Africa to combat menstrual poverty and supporting women battling cancer. She starts mentoring other entrepreneurs, launches a 6-month program called "Grace Over Grind," and speaks at the Women Who Mean Business Summit in October 2025.

From being fired three times to a multimillion-dollar brand.

That's not luck. That's what happens when you turn rejection into redirection.

Power Moves

1. Read rejection as research, not failure

Charis got fired three times. She could've taken it personally, could've believed she wasn't good enough. But after the third time, she asked a different question: What's the pattern? The pattern wasn't "I'm bad at my job." The pattern was "Corporate structures don't fit creative, bold people who think differently." That's data, not defeat.

She used that data to build differently, to create a business where her creativity was the asset, not the liability. When you get rejected, stop asking "What's wrong with me?" Start asking "What's this showing me?" Maybe the job wasn't right, maybe the industry wasn't right, maybe the whole model wasn't right. That's not failure. That's information. Use it.

2. Pivot before you're broke

Charis didn't wait for trade shows to completely fail. She saw the signs early—traveling was exhausting, sales were inconsistent, she couldn't do it with twin babies. So she pivoted before she ran out of money, before she had no options left.

Most people wait too long. They hope things will get better and push through until they collapse. Smart people shift when they see momentum slowing, when the model stops working, when the cost gets too high. Charis saw livestreaming as an experiment, not a desperate last resort. She tried it. It worked. She doubled down. That's pivot power—not waiting for crisis, but adjusting when you see the data changing.

3. Start with what you have, not what you need

Charis didn't have investor money, didn't have a fancy studio, didn't have professional equipment. She had a kitchen, a phone, jewelry, and her personality. She used that. Most people don't start because they're waiting for perfect conditions—the right funding, the right connections, the right moment. But perfect never comes.

Charis sold her car, maxed out credit cards, and built a pop-up shop in her kitchen. She worked with real resources, not ideal ones. And real resources, used well, are enough to start. You don't need everything. You just need enough to take the first step, then the second, then the third.

4. Build community, not just customers

The Sparkle Parties were not just sales events. They were connection. Charis talked to her viewers, responded to every comment, and made them feel seen, valued, and part of something. Women did not just buy jewelry, they showed up every week because they felt like they belonged.

That is what saved the business during the pandemic. When everything shut down, Sassy Jones customers did not leave. They came back every week because it was not about jewelry anymore. It was about community. When you build community, you build loyalty. And loyalty survives downturns, competition, and changes.

Do not just sell a product. Create a space where people feel like they matter. That is how you turn customers into fans, fans into advocates, and advocates into a movement.

Mind Trap

The Permanence Mind Trap: Believing rejection defines your future

Here's what stops most people after they get fired or rejected. They think: This is who I am. I'm not good enough. I'll always fail. The rejection becomes their identity—not a moment, not feedback, but their whole story. So they stop trying or they try the same thing again, hoping for different results. But nothing changes.

Why does this happen? Your brain is trying to protect you. It says: "You got hurt here. Don't go back. Don't try again. Stay safe." But safe means stuck.

The trap is believing the rejection was about your worth, your value, your capability. It wasn't. The rejection was about fit, about timing, about whether that specific place was right for you.

Charis could've believed: "I got fired three times. I'm unemployable. I'm a failure." But she didn't. She asked: "Am I the wrong person? Or was that the wrong place?" Usually, it's the wrong place.

The fix is separating rejection of your work from rejection of your worth. When someone says no to your pitch, they're not saying no to you as a person. They're saying no to that specific offer at that specific time. When a company fires you, they're not saying you're worthless. They're saying you don't fit their system. That's not a permanent truth about you. That's temporary information about them.

Charis realized corporate structures weren't built for people like her. She needed a different structure, so she built one.

Here's what happens when you reframe rejection: You stop taking it personally and start taking it strategically.

You ask: What did I learn? Where should I go instead? What should I build differently? You see rejection as redirection—not a dead end, but a turn.

Charis got fired three times. Each time pointed her toward entrepreneurship, toward building her own rules, toward Sassy Jones. The rejection wasn't punishment. It was direction.

Stop staring at the closed door. Start looking for the open window. Or build a new door yourself. That's how you escape the permanence trap—not by avoiding rejection, but by using it.

Modern Reflection

Charis built Sassy Jones starting in 2013 and pivoted to livestreaming in 2016. Back then, Facebook Live was new, livestream shopping was experimental, and most businesses did not even have strong websites yet. She was early, a pioneer.

Now it is 2025, and everything has changed. The tools are better, the platforms are bigger, and the opportunity is massive.

Here is what is different now. Livestream commerce is mainstream through TikTok Shop, Instagram Shopping, Amazon Live, and YouTube Shopping. What Charis did in her kitchen in 2016 is now a five hundred-billion-dollar industry globally. You no longer need to convince people to buy from livestreams. They already do it every day.

The creator economy is real, with more than two hundred million creators worldwide and a market worth more than one hundred billion dollars. You can build a full time business from your phone with no office, no employees, and no investors. Charis proved that it works. Now millions of people are doing it.

Getting fired matters less because job security is gone anyway. The average person changes jobs twelve times in their career, layoffs are constant, and AI is replacing many roles. The Fortune five hundred companies that fired Charis have laid off thousands. Some no longer exist. But Sassy Jones is still here, still growing, still hers. That is the advantage of building your own platform. No one can fire you, no one can lay you off, and you remain in control.

Remote work changed everything after 2020 when everyone moved online. The customers Charis was building online for four years suddenly became the customers everyone needed. While other businesses scrambled to understand digital systems, she was already there, already streaming, already connecting. The pandemic proved her model. She was not lucky. She was early.

Here is what this means for you now. You have no excuse not to start. Charis sold her car in 2015 to buy inventory. You already have a phone with a camera better than professional equipment from that year. Charis had to teach people how to buy from livestreams. You have millions of people who are already trained and comfortable buying online. Charis had Facebook Live. You have TikTok, Instagram, YouTube, LinkedIn, Substack, Patreon, Shopify, and many other platforms. The barriers are gone. The tools are free or inexpensive. The audience is waiting.

But some things have not changed. You still have to show up consistently. You still need to be real because people do not follow perfection. They follow authenticity. You still need to pivot when something stops working. And rejection is still redirection. Getting fired in 2025 might be the best thing that happens to you.

You can now build something you control, something no company can take away, something no algorithm can destroy. The question is not whether you can build your own thing. The question is why you have not started yet.

Charis started with a car trunk in 2013. You can start with a phone screen in 2025. The advantage is yours. Use it.

Charis Jones showed us what to do when systems reject you. Read the rejection as research, pivot before you are broke, and build with the resources you already have. She built Sassy Jones alone in her kitchen with twin babies, while maxing out credit cards and betting everything on her vision. And it worked.

But building alone is not the only path. Sometimes the most strategic move is not to work harder by yourself. It is to find the right partner, someone whose strengths fill your gaps, who sees what you miss, and who brings what you lack.

Two comedians in New York City figured this out. Separately, they were talented performers fighting for stage time in a crowded industry. Together, they became 2 Dope Queens and changed what was possible.

This is what happens when you stop trying to do everything alone and start building with someone who makes you better.

CHAPTER 6

FIND YOUR PEOPLE AND BUILD TOGETHER

*You don't have to rise alone.
Find your people and climb faster.*
Phoebe Robinson.

Two comedians could not get enough stage time.

Phoebe Robinson had writing and production skills, strong Brooklyn comedy connections, and a voice that was not getting heard. Jessica Williams had Daily Show credibility, comedy networks in Los Angeles, and a platform that was not big enough for what she wanted to say.

Separately, they were talented performers fighting for scraps in a crowded industry. Together, they became 2 Dope Queens, a podcast that sold out live shows, became an HBO special series, and launched both of their careers into the stratosphere.

They did not wait for comedy clubs to book them more. They did not wait for networks to give them shows. They did not wait for gatekeepers to say yes. They bought microphones, rented space in Brooklyn, and pressed record.

What made them powerful was not only their individual talent. It was the way their strengths combined. They had different networks, different skills, and different perspectives. They built their own platform, shared credit equally, and created space for other marginalized comedians who could not get booked.

And when HBO came calling, they had leverage because they had already proven that the audience existed.

This is how you find a partner whose strengths complement yours and build something neither of you could create alone.

Reader's Transition

Most people think success is solo—one person, one vision, one breakthrough. That's the myth: the lone genius, the self-made billionaire, the solo artist who needs no one. But that's not how underdogs win.

Smart underdogs know you rise faster together. Two voices reach further than one, two people pushing move the work faster, and two underdogs teaming up shift the odds. You don't have to do it all alone. You shouldn't try to.

Find your allies—people who share your drive, your vision, your values. Then build together, share the credit, share the platform, and share the wins. Because when you rise together, three things happen: You build faster because you're not carrying everything alone. You reach further because you combine audiences, skills, and networks. You create community because you're modeling collaboration over competition.

The world that says "only one person can win" becomes the world where everyone wins. Because you didn't fight for the spotlight. You built a bigger stage.

Complementary partnerships multiply impact across every industry. Phoebe and Jessica built comedy together, but the principle applies everywhere. In tech, it's the technical founder paired with the business founder. In healthcare, it's the clinician partnered with the practice administrator. In consulting, it's the strategist working with the implementation expert.

As you read their story, ask yourself: Who has the strengths that fill my gaps—and how could we build something together that neither of us could create alone?

Origin

September 28, 1984. Bedford Heights, Ohio.

Phoebe Robinson is born and grows up in Bedford Heights and later Solon, Ohio—suburbs, mostly white neighborhoods. She's a tomboy who plays sports with her older brother Phil and watches wrestling together. They're close, best friends. But school is different at Gilmour Academy, a private school in Gates Mills, where she's the only Black girl in her grade. The only one.

She describes herself as "really dorky." While other kids go to parties, Phoebe stays home watching The West

Wing, reading books, and writing stories. She's smart but a "slacker" with grades, and her parents are frustrated because they know she's capable of more. She doesn't fit in—too Black for her white classmates, too "white" for other Black kids, too dorky for the popular kids.

It's lonely being the only one, being different. But she finds escape in entertainment—TV, movies, stories—and dreams of becoming a screenwriter one day. Her brother Phil supports her, and even though they're different (he'll go into politics, she wants entertainment), they stay close. She's his biggest fan. He's hers.

College. Pratt Institute, New York City.

Phoebe studies screenwriting and finally does what she loves—learning craft, finding focus, realizing her potential. She does some improv in college for fun, but she's serious about film. That's the plan: be a screenwriter, work in the film industry.

2008. Post-college.

Phoebe is working at an indie film company, producing, writing, and building a career when a friend invites her to take a stand-up comedy class at Carolines on Broadway—eight weeks, and the friend doesn't want to go alone. Phoebe says yes only to support her friend. She's not interested in stand-up. She's a serious film writer.

First class: Phoebe holds the microphone for the first time at an open mic, and something clicks. "This is exactly what I should be doing." It feels right, natural, like coming home. She finishes the eight-week course with a final showcase of five minutes on stage.

October 2008: The indie film company where Phoebe works folds and shuts down. She's out of a job. She takes it as a sign—the universe telling her to go all in on comedy. She starts doing open mics every night in small clubs and tiny rooms with crowds that don't pay attention, people talking through her set. Bombing, learning, growing. It's hard and lonely. The rooms are mostly men, mostly white. She's often the only Black woman, sometimes the only woman period. She keeps going.

She starts a blog called "Blaria"—like a Black version of Daria, the cartoon character. It's funny, it's smart, it's her. The blog becomes a monthly live stand-up show in Brooklyn called "Blaria LIVE!" She books other comedians, creates a space, and builds community. It's small but growing. But it's still lonely. She's building alone, and she's tired of being the only one in rooms that weren't built for her.

July 31, 1989. Los Angeles County, California.

Jessica Williams is born to parents Leon and Maria. She has a sister, Daphne, and grows up in LA, attending Nathaniel Narbonne High School in Harbor City where she studies drama. She's funny, natural, and confident on stage. She makes her TV debut in 2006 on Nickelodeon's Just for Kicks at age 17, then goes to Cal State Long Beach, graduates, and performs at Upright Citizens Brigade Theatre in LA doing improv comedy.

2012: At 22, Jessica becomes a correspondent on The Daily Show—the youngest correspondent ever in the show's history. She's making it, rising fast, becoming known.

Play by Play

The meeting: July 2014.

Phoebe Robinson is hired as a background actor for a Daily Show segment that Jessica Williams is filming about Black women and their hair in the military. During downtime on set, they start talking. It is just casual conversation, but the chemistry is instant. They laugh easily, finish each other's thoughts, and understand each other's references.

Phoebe mentions that she hosts a podcast called Blaria and asks if Jessica wants to be a guest. Jessica says yes.

The podcast episode goes incredibly well. The conversation flows, the laughs are natural, and the connection is clear. Phoebe then invites Jessica to join her as a host for her live stand up show in Brooklyn called Blaria LIVE. Jessica agrees, and they have fifteen minutes to prepare backstage before walking on.

They step on stage, and it is magic. The energy, the chemistry, the rhythm between them, everything clicks. The crowd feels it. They feel it. Jessica later says it was like a great first date and that she knew she would be going home with them that night. After the show, they look at each other and both know they should build something together for real.

The pitch: Early 2016.

Phoebe and Jessica pitch a podcast to WNYC Studios, a new division looking for shows. They explain the concept: a live comedy podcast with two Black women having funny, smart, honest conversations and featuring diverse comedians who don't usually get the spotlight—women, people of color, LGBTQ comedians, voices that mainstream comedy ignores. They'll record in Brooklyn in front of a live audience, keep it real, keep it funny, keep it them.

WNYC says yes.

The launch: April 4, 2016.

2 Dope Queens launches. The first episode drops, with Phoebe and Jessica talking, laughing, and introducing other comedians, recorded at Union Hall in Brooklyn with a live audience and real energy. During the first week, the podcast reaches number one on the iTunes podcast charts and remains there for seven days.

People are hungry for this. Two Black women being funny without apologizing, without shrinking, without code switching. They are simply being themselves, loud, smart, and hilarious. The downloads pour in, and comments explode. People say things like this is what I have been waiting for, I have never heard myself in comedy before, and where has this been.

They continue making episodes recorded live with different guests each time. They feature diverse performers who have real conversations about race, dating, money, hair, and everyday life. The show grows quickly. By the end of 2016, 2 Dope Queens is one of the most popular comedy podcasts in the country.

The deal: August 10, 2017.

HBO makes it official—they're ordering four hour-long specials based on the podcast to air in 2018. Phoebe and Jessica are executive producers with creative control to make it exactly what they want. Tig Notaro will direct, and they'll record at Kings Theatre in Brooklyn—bigger venue, bigger production, but same spirit.

Breakthrough

February 2, 2018.

The HBO specials premiere with celebrity guests like Jon Stewart, Sarah Jessica Parker, Tituss Burgess, and Uzo Aduba. But it's still Phoebe and Jessica being themselves with the same chemistry and the same mission: give space to voices that don't usually get heard. The specials are a hit—critics love them, audiences love them.

July 2018: HBO orders four more episodes for Season 2.

The finale.

November 14, 2018: The podcast records its final episode—49 main episodes plus 20 bonus episodes for 69 total. The final guest? Michelle Obama, Former First Lady of the United States, on 2 Dope Queens. That's how far they've come—from Union Hall in Brooklyn to interviewing Michelle Obama.

February 8, 2019: Season 2 of the HBO specials premieres with four more episodes, and then it's done. Phoebe and Jessica decide to end the show not because it failed, but because it succeeded. Their careers have exploded with new opportunities, new projects, and new directions. It's a "champagne problem"—they're ending because they're too busy succeeding.

What they built individually.

But the breakthrough is not only the podcast or the HBO deal or the success. The breakthrough is what they built together, something neither one could have built alone.

Phoebe's career after 2 Dope Queens:

2016: She publishes her first book titled You Cannot Touch My Hair, which becomes a New York Times bestseller.

2018: She publishes *Everythings Trash, But It Is Okay*, which also becomes a New York Times bestseller.

July 2020: She launches her own publishing imprint called Tiny Reparations Books to publish diverse voices in partnership with Plume and Penguin Random House.

2021: She publishes her third book titled Please Do Not Sit on My Bed in Your Outside Clothes, a national bestseller and the first title released through her own imprint. She also premieres her interview show Doing the Most with Phoebe Robinson on Comedy Central.

2022: She premieres the television series *Everythings Trash* on Freeform based on her book, where she stars and serves as executive producer.

2024: She signs a first look television deal with Sony Pictures Television. Through her production company Tiny Reparations, she releases her second stand up special titled *I Do Not Wanna Work Anymore* on YouTube, serves as executive producer for the cooking competition series Clash the Cookbooks, and continues touring with her stand-up comedy.

Jessica's career also expands rapidly after 2 Dope Queens, through acting, producing, and building her own creative empire.

Two women who once struggled to find space in comedy clubs are now two women running their own production companies and reshaping the industry. Even more important, the foundation was created together.

2 Dope Queens proved that there was a real audience for their voices, for diverse voices, and for honest, funny, and intelligent conversations that the mainstream overlooked. The podcast became their proof, their leverage, and their platform. When Phoebe pitched books, she had evidence that people wanted her voice. When she launched a publishing imprint, she already had credibility. When she secured television deals, she brought an audience with her. The same was true for Jessica.

They did not fight for the spotlight. They built a larger stage, and from that shared stage, each of them created stages of their own.

From being the only Black girl in her grade to building a multimedia empire. From lonely open mic nights to HBO specials. From hearing there is no space for you to saying we are creating space for everyone. That is not luck. That is what happens when you find your ally and build together.

Power Moves

1. Find partners whose strengths complement yours

Phoebe brought writing, production skills, and Brooklyn comedy connections. Jessica brought TV experience, Daily Show credibility, and LA comedy connections. Together, they had what neither had alone: two different networks, two different skillsets, two different perspectives that created something bigger.

Don't look for someone exactly like you. Look for someone who fills your gaps, who sees what you miss, who brings what you lack. Then combine strengths. That's when 1+1 = 10.

2. Build your own platform together

Phoebe and Jessica didn't wait for comedy clubs to book them more, didn't wait for networks to give them shows, didn't wait for gatekeepers to say yes. They built their own platform—a podcast recorded in Brooklyn and posted online with no budget, no corporate backing, just two women, microphones, and a mission.

That platform became their proof. When HBO came calling, they had leverage because they'd already built an audience and already proven the concept worked. You don't need permission to create. You need a partner and a platform.

3. Share credit and success openly

2 Dope Queens never became "The Phoebe Show" or "The Jessica Show." It stayed "2 Dope Queens"—cohosts,

co-creators, co-executive producers. They shared credit equally and celebrated each other publicly. When one won, they both won.

That generosity created loyalty and trust—a partnership that could handle success without jealousy. Share ownership, not just the wins but the work too, the decisions, the risks, and the rewards. When everyone shines, the whole project glows.

4. Create community, not just content

Phoebe and Jessica did not simply make a funny podcast. They created a space. They featured comedians who could not get booked elsewhere and gave them stage time, a platform, and real exposure. They highlighted women, people of color, LGBTQ comedians, and voices the mainstream ignored. They proved there is room for everyone. Your win does not have to be my loss.

That community became their strength. When they needed support, the community showed up. When they launched new projects, the community amplified them. Build for your people. Make space for others. Create community, not only audience.

Mind Trap

The Solo Hero Mind Trap: Thinking you have to do it all alone

Here's what stops people from collaborating. They think: "If I share credit, I get less. If I partner up, I'm not self-made. If I need help, I'm weak." That's the American Dream lie—the myth of the self-made individual, the solo hero who needs no one. It's everywhere in movies, books, and business stories: "I did it all myself." But it's a lie. No one succeeds alone. Ever.

Why does this happen? Because culture teaches us that needing help is weakness, that asking for support is failure, that sharing credit means you didn't really earn it. So people stay isolated, carry everything alone, burn out, struggle, and give up—all because they're afraid that partnering up means they're not "really" successful.

Here's the truth: Solo isn't stronger. It's slower.

Phoebe could have kept doing Blaria alone, built it slowly over years, and maybe made it work eventually. But partnering with Jessica accelerated everything—combined audiences, combined skills, combined networks. They went from small podcast to HBO in two years. Would that have happened solo? Maybe, eventually, but much slower.

Jessica could have pitched her own show, used her Daily Show credentials, and built something alone. But partnering with Phoebe gave her a creative outlet she couldn't get at Daily Show, a platform to be fully herself, and a partnership that became friendship.

The fix is changing your definition of success: Success isn't "I did it all alone." Success is "I built something that matters, and I did it with people who made it better." Success isn't hoarding credit—it's sharing it and watching the impact multiply. Success isn't proving you don't need anyone—it's finding the right people and building something neither of you could build alone.

Stop trying to be the solo hero. Start looking for your allies. Because the fastest way to rise is together.

Modern Reflection

When Phoebe and Jessica started 2 Dope Queens in 2016, podcasting was still relatively new—a few big shows, but not yet mainstream. Now, in 2025, everything has changed.

Collaboration is the currency of the creator economy. Podcasts are everywhere, along with YouTube channels, TikTok duos, co-hosted newsletters, Instagram collabs, and LinkedIn partnerships. The most successful creators aren't solo acts—they're partnerships, collaborations, and networks.

Why? Because collaboration compounds growth. When two creators partner up, they don't just add their audiences (100 + 100 = 200). They multiply them (100 x 100 = 10,000) because each person's audience discovers the other.

The tools make collaboration easier than ever. In 2016, Phoebe and Jessica had to be in the same room to record, find a venue, and coordinate schedules. Now? You can record with someone across the world using Zoom, Riverside, SquadCast, or StreamYard. You can edit together remotely, share files instantly, and collaborate asynchronously. The barrier isn't logistics anymore. It's mindset.

The algorithm rewards collaboration. YouTube promotes videos with multiple creators. Instagram loves collab posts. TikTok pushes duets. Podcasts with guests perform better than solo shows. Why? Because collaboration equals more engagement, more comments, more shares, and more growth. The platforms want you to collaborate—they built features for it.

But some things haven't changed: You still need the right partner—someone who shares your values, your work ethic, your vision. You still need to share credit generously with no ego and no competition, just genuine partnership. You still need to show up consistently because collaboration doesn't work if one person does all the work.

Here's what this means for you: You have no excuse not to find a partner. The tools exist, the platforms reward it, and the audience wants it. Find someone doing similar work in a different way, someone whose audience complements yours, someone you genuinely enjoy working with.

Then create something together—a podcast, a video series, a newsletter, a product, a service. Split everything

50/50: credit, work, decisions, and revenue. Show up consistently, support each other publicly, and build together. And watch what happens when two underdogs team up.

Phoebe Robinson and Jessica Williams built 2 Dope Queens in four years. Four years from a Brooklyn apartment to HBO specials, four years from nobody knows us to sold out shows and cultural impact. That is lightning fast.

But not every path moves at that pace. And that is okay. Sometimes the breakthrough takes longer, much longer. Sometimes you stack small wins for five years, then ten years, then fifteen years, and nobody knows your name.

The world calls it overnight success when you finally break through. But you know the truth. There was nothing overnight about it. Every small role, every audition, every year of practice, none of it was wasted time. It was building time.

Viola Davis understands this more than almost anyone. For fifteen years, she worked in roles most people would forget. But those fifteen years created something the world could not ignore.

This is what patient, persistent, compound progress looks like.

PART III
CREATE YOUR OWN DOOR

When opportunity doesn't knock, build the entrance yourself.

By now, you've learned how to start without permission.

You've learned how to stay when the noise fades. Now comes the most powerful step — *creating your own door.*

This is where underdogs stop asking to be seen and start designing their own visibility. Where they turn the proof they've built into platforms, partnerships, and possibilities, and waiting is no longer part of the strategy.

Few people reach this point. They start, but don't finish. They build, but don't share. They make progress but stay quiet about it. Or they keep waiting for the right person to notice; a boss, an investor, a gatekeeper, someone to say, "It's your turn." People who build their own doors don't wait for turns. They *create momentum that can't be ignored.*

Creating your own door isn't about arrogance or ego. It's about ownership. It's realizing that the proof you've built gives you the right to design your next opportunity — to walk into rooms you once only dreamed of, or to create entirely new ones.

The people in this section did just that. Some launched new companies after being told they weren't "ready." Some built communities from the ground up when no one would sponsor them, and some created platforms that gave voice to others still waiting outside.

They didn't ask for permission. They built systems that made permission irrelevant.

This is where courage meets creativity. Where your experience becomes leverage, and where your story becomes strategy. Once you've stacked wins and built proof, the next move isn't to ask, "Will someone open a door for me?" It's to ask, *"Which one will I build next?"*

Your ideas are the blueprint. Your proof is the material, and your consistency is the hammer. So, build boldly, build for others and build something that can't be ignored.

Create your own door — and make sure it never closes behind you.

CHAPTER 7

STACK SMALL WINS INTO BIG BREAKTHROUGHS

Build your proof one victory at a time.
— Viola Davis

For fifteen years, Viola Davis auditioned, worked, and waited. Theater roles, bit parts, one-line appearances, small paychecks, smaller recognition. Her friends were getting famous, landing series, and signing movie deals.

Viola kept showing up, kept working, and kept stacking small wins that most people would forget.

Nobody knew her name.

Then, in 2008, she walked onto a film set and performed one scene—eight minutes—in *Doubt*. Those eight minutes earned her an Oscar nomination. But that scene wasn't eight minutes. It was fifteen years. Every theater performance, every bit part, every audition, every acting class, every year of practice. They stacked, one on top of another, building, growing, and compounding.

Until one day, the stack was tall enough to reach the breakthrough that looked like overnight success.

Most people quit after five years, after ten. They think, "It's not working. I'm not getting anywhere." Viola worked for fifteen years before her breakthrough. And those fifteen years didn't slow her down. They built her.

This is how small wins compound into moments that change everything.

Reader's Transition

Some people wait for one big break—one lucky moment, one person to discover them and change everything. That's not how it works.

Real success is built from small wins—tiny victories, moments nobody sees, work nobody celebrates. Each small win teaches you something, builds your skill, proves you can do it, and gives you confidence for the next one. Then you stack another win on top, and another, and another.

Until one day, you look up and realize you're not the same person who started. You're stronger, better, and ready. You don't wait for the big moment. You create it by stacking small moments.

Every audition teaches you something. Every role makes you better. Every rejection sharpens you. Every small victory builds momentum. You can't skip the small wins—they're not just steps on the way to success. They ARE the success.

Because when your big moment finally comes, it's not luck. It's proof. Proof that you've been building toward this for years, one small win at a time.

Compound progress builds credibility across every industry. Viola stacked roles for 15 years in

entertainment, but the principle applies everywhere. In tech, it's years of contributing to open source before the

CTO offer. In healthcare, it's a decade of refining your approach before national recognition. In consulting, it's years of client work before you're the go-to industry expert.

As you read Viola's story, ask yourself: What small win can I achieve this month that, stacked with next month's win, builds toward something breakthrough in 5-10 years?

Origin

August 11, 1965. St. Matthews, South Carolina.

Viola Davis is born on a former plantation called Singleton Plantation, the same land where her ancestors were enslaved. Her grandfather is a sharecropper, and many of her uncles and cousins work as farmers because that is the only option available to them. Her grandmother lives in a one room shack with no running water and no bathroom, only an outhouse.

But on the day Viola is born, the house is full. Aunts and uncles are drinking and laughing, and her mother eats a sardine, mustard, onion, and tomato sandwich after giving birth. It is celebration in the middle of poverty, joy inside a decimated environment. That is what Viola remembers.

She is the second youngest of six children, four sisters and one brother, and her parents cannot afford to keep all of them together. Soon after Viola is born, her parents move her and two older siblings to Central Falls in Rhode Island, while the other children remain with their grandparents in South Carolina. The family is divided, but Viola at least has a chance at something different.

Central Falls is not much better. It is still poor and still struggling. Her mother is a civil rights activist, and when Viola is two years old, her mother is arrested at a protest. Viola goes to jail with her. That is her childhood, a life shaped by poverty, hunger, cold, and a constant fight for something more.

But Viola has something within her, a fire, an intensity, a hunger that is not only about food. She wants more. She knows there is something beyond Central Falls, beyond poverty, beyond what people expect from a poor Black girl from Rhode Island. She just does not know what it is yet.

Play by Play

High school: The first brick.

Viola discovers acting, not on purpose. A teacher notices her, the way she carries herself, the intensity in her eyes, the way she can hold silence like a weapon. The teacher puts her in a play and gives her a stage. That tiny stage in Central Falls becomes the first brick in a wall Viola does not know she is building yet.

She is good, really good, but she is poor and her family cannot afford acting classes or theater camps. She joins Upward Bound, a federal program that helps low income students prepare for college, and they help her apply for scholarships. She gets into the Young Peoples School for the Performing Arts with a scholarship, trains there, learns, and grows. Then she attends Rhode Island College with another scholarship, where she studies theater and performs with the Trinity Repertory Company.

She is talented, everyone can see it, but talent is not enough. She needs training, real training. A friend tells her,

apply to Juilliard, Yale, New York University, and the State University of New York at Purchase. Viola looks at the application fees. She can afford only one. She chooses Juilliard, the best drama school in the world. One application. One shot.

1989. The audition.

Viola is 23 years old and still performing in a play in Rhode Island when she travels to New York for her Juilliard audition. The standard audition is a multi-day process, but Viola doesn't have multiple days—she has work, bills, and a long commute. She asks for an immediate decision, right there, right now.

The professors gather and watch her perform a monologue from *The Color Purple*. They see the raw talent, the passion, the strength and fire. They accept her on the spot—one of fourteen accepted out of 2,500 applicants.

She gets a full scholarship for four years, 1989 to 1993. A poor girl from Central Falls is going to Juilliard. **1993. The long build begins.**

Viola leaves Juilliard ready to conquer the world—trained, talented, and ready. The world is not. She starts auditioning for Broadway, Off-Broadway, TV, and film. Anything. She gets small roles, theater productions that don't pay much, and parts so small they barely count as credits. She works steadily, but steadily doesn't mean successfully. It means surviving.

1996: Viola gets her Screen Actors Guild card from one day of work on a film called *The Substance of Fire*. She plays a nurse who hands a vial of blood to another actor. She gets paid $518. That's it—one day, five hundred dollars, years after Juilliard. Most people would quit, would say, "This isn't working. I should do something else." Viola keeps going.

She does bit parts on TV—*NYPD Blue*, *New York Undercover*, *The Pentagon Wars* on HBO. She takes any role she can get, not because they're good roles, but because she needs to work, because each role teaches her something.

Late 1990s to early 2000s: Building in the margins.

Viola becomes a force in theater with powerful performances in *Intimate Apparel* and *King Hedley II*. Critics notice—she's formidable. But her film and TV profile stays low. She's working, but she's not breaking through.

She appears in films by good directors—Steven Soderbergh, George Clooney, Oliver Stone—in *Out of Sight*, *Traffic*, *Solaris*, *Syriana*, and *World Trade Center*. But always in small roles, supporting parts, background characters. She's in *Kate & Leopold*, *Far from Heaven*, and *Antwone Fisher*—good films, small roles. She gets recurring work on *Law & Order: SVU* and starring roles in two TV series that get canceled quickly: *Traveler* and *Century City*.

Years pass. She's working steadily, but she's not famous, she's not rich, and she's not breaking through. Every audition is a small win. Every role is practice. Every performance builds her craft. She's stacking wins, one at a time. Nobody's counting but her.

2008. Fifteen years after Juilliard.

Viola hears that *Doubt*, a Pulitzer Prize-winning play, is being adapted into a film with Meryl Streep attached—a prestige project. The producer, Scott Rudin, already knows Viola's work and likes it. But Viola doesn't wait for them to call her. She calls her manager: "Get me an audition." Not "Can you get me an audition?" Just: "Get me an audition."

She auditions in Los Angeles, gets a callback in New York, then a screen test with six other Black actresses all competing for one role—Mrs. Miller, a grieving mother with one scene and maybe ten minutes of screen time.

Full costume, full hair and makeup, performing in front of producers, director John Patrick Shanley, and the full crew.

Viola knows this is it—the moment everything's been building toward. She performs the scene, pouring fifteen years of invisible work into ten minutes. One hour and thirty minutes later, they offer her the role.

Breakthrough

Doubt releases in 2008.

Viola Davis has one scene—ten minutes, no glamour, no makeup, just raw emotion. A mother fighting for her son. The room goes still when she performs, then the applause starts.

Roger Ebert, the famous film critic, writes: "It lasts about 10 minutes, but it is the emotional heart and soul of

Doubt, and if Viola Davis isn't nominated by the Academy, an injustice will have been done."

She gets nominated—Oscar, Golden Globe, Screen Actors Guild Award. After fifteen years of small roles, bit parts, and canceled TV shows, Viola Davis is an Oscar nominee. But she doesn't stop there.

The cascade of recognition.

2010: She returns to Broadway in *Fences* and wins her second Tony Award as the second African American woman to win Best Leading Actress in a Play.

2011: She stars in *The Help*, gets her second Oscar nomination, wins two SAG Awards, and Time magazine lists her as one of the most influential people in the world.

2014: She's cast in *How to Get Away with Murder* as the lead—Annalise Keating, a tough criminal defense attorney.

2015: She wins the Emmy for Outstanding Lead Actress in a Drama Series, the first African American woman to win that award.

2016: She reprises her role in *Fences* for the film version and wins the Academy Award for Best Supporting Actress. With that win, Viola Davis becomes the first African American to achieve the "Triple Crown of Acting": an Oscar, an Emmy, and a Tony.

2020: *Ma Rainey's Black Bottom* brings her fourth Oscar nomination, and she becomes the most nominated Black actress in Oscar history.

2022: Her memoir *Finding Me* wins a Grammy for Best Audiobook, and she achieves EGOT status—Emmy, Grammy, Oscar, Tony. She's one of the few performers in history to win all four.

From a one-room shack with no running water to EGOT. From $518 for one day of work to the most nominated Black actress ever. From fifteen years of small roles to the pinnacle of her profession.

That's not luck. That's stacking wins, one small victory at a time, for decades. Until the stack becomes unstoppable.

Power Moves

1. Celebrate every small win to build momentum

Viola didn't just collect small wins—she used them. Each bit part taught her something, each audition sharpened her, and each role built her confidence. Small wins release dopamine in your brain, the chemical that makes you feel good and tells you: "Do that again."

That's why small wins matter. They don't just move you forward—they make you want to keep moving. You don't need the big break yet. You need the small win today, then another tomorrow. Stack them. They compound.

2. Document every victory as proof you're building

For fifteen years, Viola worked in roles most people would forget, but she didn't forget. She kept building her resume, her reel, her proof. Every role went on her credits, every performance added to her body of work, and every review showed her growth.

By the time *Doubt* came around, she had proof. She wasn't an unknown—she was a working actress with fifteen years of credits. Keep a record of your wins, not to brag but to build, to show yourself and others: I'm not starting from zero. I'm building. Write them down. Track them. Save them. They're your receipts.

3. Trust slow progress over quick wins

Most people quit after five years, after ten. They think, "It's not working. I'm not getting anywhere." Viola worked for fifteen years before her breakthrough—fifteen years of small roles, small paychecks, and small recognition. But slow isn't failure. Slow is strategic.

Slow progress protects quality. It gives time for skill to mature, for judgment to develop, for credibility to build.

If Viola had gotten famous at 25, would she have been ready? Would she have had the depth to do that scene in *Doubt*? No. She needed those fifteen years. They built her. Trust the slow build. It's preparing you for what's coming.

4. Stack micro-wins until they become breakthrough moments

Viola's Oscar nomination for *Doubt* wasn't one moment. It was a thousand moments—every theater performance, every bit part, every audition, every role, every year of practice. They stacked, one on top of another, building, growing, and compounding. Until one day, the stack was tall enough to reach the breakthrough.

That's how it works. You don't get one big win. You get a thousand small wins that become one big moment. Keep stacking.

Mind Trap

The Impatience Mind Trap: Quitting right before the breakthrough

Here's what happens to most people. They start building, work hard, and make progress. But the progress is slow, too slow, and they can't see results yet. So they think: "This isn't working. I'm wasting my time. I should try something else." They quit, right before the breakthrough.

Viola could have quit in 1998—five years after Juilliard, still doing bit parts, still making $518 for one day of work.

She could have quit in 2003—ten years after Juilliard, still not famous, still not breaking through. She could have quit in 2007, the year before *Doubt*—still waiting, still hoping, still stacking small wins that nobody was counting. But she didn't quit. She kept going—one more year, one more audition, one more role. And in 2008, everything changed.

Why does this happen? Because your brain wants instant results. It doesn't understand compound growth and doesn't see the wins stacking beneath the surface. All your brain sees is: "I worked hard. Nothing changed. This isn't working." But that's a lie. Something IS changing. You're getting better, building proof, and preparing. You're just in the boring middle—the phase where nothing looks different on the outside but everything is strengthening underneath.

This is the plateau, the period where effort stays the same but visible results seem flat. Most people quit here because they think the plateau means failure. But the plateau is preparation—your skills are maturing, your judgment is developing, and your foundation is solidifying.

Here's the truth: Breakthroughs look sudden, but they're not. They're the result of thousands of hours of invisible work finally becoming visible. Viola's breakthrough in *Doubt* looked sudden—one scene, one nomination, one moment. But it wasn't sudden. It was fifteen years of preparation meeting one open door.

The fix is trusting the stack: You can't see all your small wins stacked up. They're invisible and feel like nothing. But they're there—building, growing, and compounding. Every audition you do, every skill you practice, every piece of work you complete—it's stacking.

You do not need to see the whole stack yet. You only need to add to it today. One more win, one more rep, one more step. Then tomorrow, do it again. Because you are not building for today. You are building for the day when someone opens a door and asks, are you ready. And you will be able to say yes, not because you got lucky, but because you have been stacking wins for years.

The breakthrough is not happening to you. It is happening through you, one layer at a time. Do not quit in the boring middle. That is where breakthroughs are built.

Modern Reflection

The old model of success was work hard, wait your turn, and hope someone notices. That still exists, but something has changed. Now you can document your progress publicly.

Viola worked for fifteen years before anyone outside theater circles knew her name. She stacked wins in the dark. Today, you can stack wins in public through social media, YouTube, newsletters, podcasts, and portfolios. You do not have to wait for a gatekeeper to say you are ready. You can show your work, build your proof, and let people watch you grow.

Every video you post is a small win. Every article you write, every project you share, is proof that you are building.

The danger is comparison. You see someone go viral overnight and think, why not me, why am I moving so slowly. But going viral is not better than growing slowly. Viral is unstable. Slow is solid.

The overnight success myth is more visible now and more damaging. TikTok stars, influencers with millions of followers, entrepreneurs claiming they made six figures in six months, it all looks instant and easy, and it makes your slow progress feel like failure.

But most overnight success stories are lies or incomplete. They do not show the years of work before the viral moment or the skills built in private. Violas Oscar nomination looked instant, but it took fifteen years. Do not compare your first year to someone else's fifteenth year. You are not behind. You are building.

The advantage today is that you can track and share your wins. Keep a log, a document, a portfolio, or a social media profile that shows your progress, not to show off, but to build proof for yourself and for others. Every small project you finish, every skill you learn, every problem you solve, document it.

When someone asks what you have been working on, you have receipts. When you doubt yourself, you can look back and see that you have been stacking. You are not stuck. You are growing.

Here is what has not changed. You still have to do the work. You still have to stack the wins. You still have to trust the slow build. The tools are different, the visibility is different, but the process is the same. Small wins, stacked consistently over time, until they become undeniable.

Viola Davis stacked small wins for fifteen years. She documented every role, built a cumulative portfolio, and trusted that slow progress was still progress. And when her moment came, she was ready, not because she got lucky, but because she had been building all along.

But here is the next question. Once you have built something valuable, once you have stacked those wins, documented that proof, and accumulated that experience, how do you make sure you get paid for it.

Too many people build incredible value and then undersell themselves. They apologize for their prices, negotiate with feelings instead of facts, and walk into rooms like guests instead of partners. Viola built the skills that earned her an Oscar, but building the skill is only half the equation. The other half is claiming the value you have created.

Janice Bryant Howroyd mastered both halves. She built a billion dollar staffing empire. But long before the billions, she mastered something more fundamental, how to track her wins like receipts, how to walk into negotiations with data instead of hope, and how to state her price with confidence instead of apology.

This is how you turn years of building into the compensation you deserve.

CHAPTER 8

KNOW YOUR WORTH AND NAME YOUR PRICE

Decide your value before the world does.
Janice Bryant Howroyd.

Janice Bryant Howroyd started a staffing agency with **$1,500** and a phone, with no office, no employees, and no fancy business plan. She had a sharp mind, a willingness to work, and complete certainty about her value.

She cold called companies, placed candidates, and tracked every metric. When clients tried to underpay her, she did not accept it quietly. She walked into negotiations with numbers. She said, **my placements stay 90 percent longer than the industry average**, and that saves you **$X** in recruitment costs and **$Y** in productivity loss. This is what that is worth.

Not feelings. Not I work really hard. Not I have been here a long time. Facts. Data. Value created. Value deserved.

Janice built Act One Group into a billion-dollar enterprise, the largest woman owned and minority owned staffing company in the United States. But long before the billions, she mastered something even more valuable, how to walk into a room like a partner rather than a guest, how to state her price without apology, and how to prove her worth with receipts.

This is how you track your value, bring data to negotiations, and claim what you have earned.

Reader's Transition

Most people wait for others to tell them what they're worth. They wait for the raise, the promotion, the recognition, the validation. They hope someone notices their hard work, sees their value, and decides to pay them fairly. They're still waiting.

Smart underdogs don't wait. They decide their worth themselves, then they prove it, then they name their price. You don't get paid what you're worth. You get paid what you negotiate. And you can't negotiate well if you don't know your value first.

When you walk into a room knowing your worth—with proof, with confidence, with clarity—everything changes. People stop questioning you and start respecting you, not because you demanded it but because you demonstrated it.

You don't need permission to be valuable. You need results, documentation, and the courage to state your price. Because when you know your worth before the world does, you stop asking for what you deserve. You start stating what you've earned.

Measuring value creates negotiating power across every industry. Janice tracked staffing metrics, but the principle applies everywhere. In tech, it's documenting the system performance improvements and cost savings you've delivered. In healthcare, it's tracking your patient outcome improvements compared to practice averages.

In creative fields, it's measuring the engagement rates and ROI your campaigns generate.

As you read Janice's story, ask yourself: What value am I creating right now that I'm not tracking—and how would documenting it change my next negotiation?

Origin

September 1, 1952. Tarboro, North Carolina.

Janice Bryant is born, the fourth of eleven children. Eleven kids in one house. Her parents run the household like a business, and they have to, since eleven children require organization, discipline, and structure. Older siblings mentor younger ones, everyone has responsibilities, and everyone contributes. The family works as a system.

Janice's grandparents run a makeshift barbecue restaurant, and her parents show her how to make things work with limited resources. The lessons are clear. Attitude beats aptitude, innovation beats complaining, and always help the next person behind you. Janice's mother teaches her the take two principle, which means always take enough to share with others.

These are not only family values. They are business principles. Janice does not know it yet, but she is getting her first MBA in that crowded house.

Teenage years. Segregated Tarboro.

Everything in Tarboro is segregated—schools, restaurants, water fountains, bathrooms. Black students attend underfunded schools while white students get the resources. When Janice is a teenager, integration begins, and she's among the first Black students to attend the previously all-white high school.

It's hostile—racist students, racist teachers. She walks through hallways where people don't want her there. **U.S. History class.**

Janice is 16, sitting in class when the teacher—a white man—stands on his desk and defends slavery, explaining why it was "appropriate" for Black people. He doesn't say "Black people." He uses worse words.

Janice sits there, biting the inside of her jaw, holding back tears, refusing to cry, refusing to give him the satisfaction. She goes home crying anyway. Her father gives her three choices: "I can go to the school and confront him. You can transfer to the all-Black high school. Or you can go back."

Janice chooses to go back. She returns to that class, sits through it, and proves him wrong by succeeding.

The textbook problem.

The Black students get textbooks, but pages are torn out—key information missing. Janice complains to her father: "How am I supposed to learn when they give us books with missing pages?" Her father doesn't coddle her. He challenges her: "Figure out what's missing."

Her mother takes it further: "Find the information. Write it down. Tape it into the book for the next student." That lesson sticks. You don't just overcome obstacles for yourself. You make it easier for the next person. **1970-1974. North Carolina A&T State University.**

Janice earns a full scholarship, studies English, and graduates with her degree. She proved the racist teacher wrong, proved she belonged, and proved she was capable. But she still doesn't know what she wants to do with her life—just that she wants more than Tarboro offers.

Play by Play

1976. Los Angeles, California.

Janice visits her sister in Los Angeles, just a visit, a vacation. Her brother in law, Tom Noonan, works at Billboard magazine and gets Janice a temporary secretarial job while she is visiting. It is supposed to be temporary, but

Janice is good, really good, organized, efficient, and a problem solver. Billboard does not want her to leave.

While working there, Janice notices something. Many of her coworkers in support roles are aspiring performers, actors, singers, and musicians. They see their jobs as temporary, only until they make it. They are not invested in the work and not aligned with the company's needs.

Janice sees the gap, the mismatch. Companies need committed employees. Employees need jobs that align with their goals. What if there is a better way to connect people with work, not just matching skills but matching goals, values, and culture.

Tom notices Janice's talent for matching people to jobs and tells her, you should start your own staffing agency. Janice thinks about it. She is good at this, she sees the opportunity, and she decides this is what she will do.

1978. Starting ACT-1.

Janice has $1,500—she borrowed $900 from her mother. She rents a small office, not a real office but the front of a rug store in Beverly Hills. She has a telephone and a phone book. That's it. No computer, no fax machine— she has to borrow a fax when she needs one.

Tom Noonan becomes her first client when Billboard hires through her agency. Janice's philosophy is different from other staffing agencies—she makes "the candidate the center of our universe." She focuses on the person, not just the position: What are their goals? What do they care about? What kind of culture fits them?

When she places someone well, they stay, perform, and thrive. The company wins, the employee wins, and Janice wins. But it's hard—really hard.

Banks won't give her loans. She's a Black woman starting a business, and they don't take her seriously. Potential clients doubt her. Some make racist comments, some make sexist comments—"stunningly insensitive remarks," she'll later say. She learns to depersonalize it, to not let it stop her, and to focus on the work, not the insults.

She remembers her father's lessons about the teacher who defended slavery, the choice to go back, and the choice to prove them wrong through results, not arguments.

She offers clients a money-back guarantee: "I'll find you the right person or I'll refund your payment." This gives her powerful incentive to make good matches and builds trust—clients know she's confident. She markets through "WOMB"—Word of Mouth, Baby! When she does good work, clients tell others, and referrals build her business.

1980s. Growing and adapting.

The economy shifts with layoffs, and companies stop hiring full-time. Janice adapts by adding temporary staffing and flexible placements—whatever clients need. She adds new divisions based on client requests: background checks, technology solutions, whatever they need.

The business grows slowly and steadily, one satisfied client at a time.

1990. Moving headquarters.

ACT-1 moves to Torrance, California—a real headquarters with real offices and real growth. Janice develops proprietary technology called "Acceleration," a system that provides detailed reporting on employees.

Companies offer to buy the technology, but she says no. Instead, she offers it as a service to clients, giving her a competitive advantage.

2000s. Going global.

ACT-1 becomes the ActOne Group and expands internationally to Canada, Denmark, Brazil, the United Kingdom—nineteen countries total. New brands emerge: AgileOne (workforce management), AppleOne (staffing), A-Check Global (background checks). Over 17,000 clients worldwide.

Breakthrough

2018. The milestone.

The Act One Group surpasses $1 billion in annual revenue. Janice Bryant Howroyd becomes the first African American woman to own and operate a company with more than $1 billion in revenue, not through inheritance, not through marriage, but by building it herself from $1,500 and a rug store office.

But the breakthrough is not only the billion dollars. It is what came before. Janice did not wait to be validated before she set her prices. She decided her worth based on the value she created. She tracked results, documented wins, and proved her impact.

When clients tried to lowball her, she did not get defensive. She showed them the math. She said, here is what it costs you when positions stay empty, here is the retention rate of my placements, here is the time I save you, here is the value I create.

She negotiated from data, not hope. From proof, not feelings. And when people doubted her because of her race, her gender, or her background, she did not argue. She delivered. Results silence doubt better than words ever can.

2021.

The Act One Group reports more than $3 billion in annual revenue. From $1,500 to $3 billion. From a rug store to nineteen countries.

2025. Still building.

At 72 years old, Janice is still CEO, still leading, still innovating. In July 2025, ActOne launches "Assembly Orchestration"—an AI-enabled process automation platform combining AI with human expertise. She hosts a podcast called "Ask JBH," sharing business advice and interviewing leaders. She serves on boards including Harvard Women's Leadership Board, United Way Worldwide, and North Carolina A&T State University Board of Trustees. She advocates for STEM education for women and minorities.

From the girl with torn textbook pages to the CEO of a multi-billion-dollar company. From segregated Tarboro to global business leader. From being told she doesn't belong to building a company that serves 17,000 clients worldwide.

That's not luck. That's what happens when you know your worth and refuse to accept anything less.

Power Moves

1. Track your wins like receipts

Janice didn't hope clients would notice her value—she documented it. Placement retention rates, time to fill positions, cost savings, client satisfaction. She kept records and built proof. When she walked into negotiations, she had numbers: "My placements stay 90% longer than industry average. That saves you recruitment costs and productivity loss."

That's not bragging. That's reporting. You can't prove your value without tracking it. Every week, document what you accomplished, what changed because of it, and any numbers, feedback, or results. Build your proof portfolio. It's your negotiating power.

2. Bring numbers, not feelings, to negotiations

Most people negotiate with feelings: "I work really hard." "I've been here a long time." "I deserve more." Janice negotiated with facts: "I created X value. That's worth Y compensation."

When you bring numbers, you're not asking for a favor—you're proposing a fair exchange. Time saved, money earned, problems solved, efficiency gained. Numbers build courage. When you know you saved a company $200K, asking for $20K more doesn't feel greedy. It feels fair.

3. Negotiate as partners, not guests

Janice never walked into meetings like she was lucky to be there. She walked in as a problem solver—not arrogant, just clear: "I have solutions. Let's discuss how we can work together."

That's the mindset shift. You're not a guest hoping for approval. You're a partner offering value. Replace "I'm grateful for the opportunity" with "I'm excited to deliver results." One sounds like you're below them. The other sounds like you're beside them. When you act like a partner, people treat you like one.

4. State your price with confidence, not apology

Janice offered a money-back guarantee. She was that confident in her value. When clients questioned her rates, she didn't defend nervously. She stated them clearly: "This is the rate for this level of service. It reflects the quality and results you'll receive."

No apology. No justification. Just clarity. Confidence doesn't mean arrogance. It means knowing what you're worth and stating it without flinching. When you apologize for your price, people hear "I'm not sure I'm worth this." When you state it confidently, they hear "This is the value."

Mind Trap

The Worthiness Mind Trap: Waiting for others to tell you what you're worth

Here is what stops most people from negotiating well. They think their worth comes from external validation. They wait for the boss to notice, the client to appreciate, the market to recognize. They think, I cannot ask for more until someone tells me I am valuable.

So they underprice, undercharge, and undervalue themselves, waiting for permission to be worth more.

Why does this happen. Because society teaches certain people that their value is up for debate. Women are told not to be too demanding. People of color face assumptions about their capabilities. People without advanced degrees doubt their expertise.

It is called imposter syndrome. Even when you have proven yourself, you feel like a fraud, like you got lucky, like someone is going to figure out that you do not really belong. Janice felt this. She has said it herself, one of her biggest internal obstacles was her own lack of belief that she could successfully run a company.

But here is what she learned. Worth is not something others give you. It is something you decide for yourself.

The truth is this. Your worth is not determined by who validates you. It is determined by the value you create. Janice did not wait for white business owners to tell her she was valuable. She created value, documented it, then priced it fairly. When people tried to underpay her, she did not accept it because she was grateful for the opportunity. She showed them the math, the results, and the proof. Her worth was not up for negotiation. Only her rate was.

The fix is shifting the question. Do not ask, am I worthy of this price. Ask, what value am I creating, what is a fair price for that value. Then document the value, calculate the impact, and state the price.

If they say no, that is data. Either they cannot afford your value, which means they are the wrong client, or you need to show the value more clearly, which is a communication issue. But do not lower your price because you doubt your worth. Lower your price only if the value does not match.

Janice offered a money back guarantee because she was certain of her value. She had proven it. She knew what she delivered. That is not arrogance. That is earned confidence.

Stop waiting for someone to tell you what you are worth. Decide it. Prove it. State it. Then build a billion-dollar life on that foundation.

Modern Reflection

When Janice started ACT-1 in 1978, salary information was secret. People didn't talk about money, and asking what someone earned was rude. This benefited employers and kept workers underpaid, especially women and people of color.

Now, in 2025, everything is changing.

Salary transparency is becoming law. More states require companies to post salary ranges in job listings— Colorado, California, New York, Washington. This levels the playing field. You can see what a role pays before you apply and research what others in your position earn. The secrecy that kept people underpaid is ending.

Remote work changed negotiation dynamics. Before: "This is what we pay for this role in this city." Now: "I can work from anywhere. I can compare offers globally." Geographic salary differences matter less when work is remote. You can negotiate based on value, not location.

Salary information is everywhere. Glassdoor, Levels.fyi, LinkedIn, Reddit, Twitter threads—people share what they earn, what they negotiated, what worked. You don't have to guess anymore. You can research. You can know what fair looks like.

But some things haven't changed: You still have to ask. Transparency helps, but negotiation still requires courage. The information is there—you have to use it. You still need proof. Knowing market rates helps, but personal proof is stronger. "Here's what I've delivered" beats "here's what others earn." You still have to know your worth first. All the data in the world won't help if you don't believe you deserve fair pay.

Here's what this means for you: You have fewer excuses than Janice had in **1978**. She built a billion-dollar company with a phone book and a borrowed fax machine. You have salary databases, remote work options, legal requirements for transparency, and online communities sharing negotiation tactics.

The tools exist. The information exists. The only question is; will you use them.

Research your worth. Document your value. State your price. Negotiate fairly. Because the world is finally catching up to what Janice knew in **1978**. Worth is not a secret. It is a calculation. Calculate yours. Then claim it.

Janice Bryant Howroyd showed us how to negotiate when you have built something valuable. Track your metrics. Bring data. Position yourself as a partner. State your worth clearly.

When you have proof of your value, negotiation becomes easier, not easy, but easier.

But what happens when you cannot negotiate. When you bring all the data, make the perfect pitch, show undeniable proof, and they still say no.

What do you do when the door stays locked? When thirty people say no, then thirty-one, then thirty-two. Most people quit long before thirty-two.

Cathy Hughes did not.

She needed a loan to buy a radio station. She had the business plan, the experience, the vision, the proof. Thirty-two banks said no anyway.

Janice's lesson was about negotiating your value when people recognize it. Cathy's lesson is about what to do when they do not, when all the data in the world is not enough, when you have to build despite rejection, not after it.

This is what relentless persistence, sharpened by adaptation, looks like.

CHAPTER 9

BUILD YOUR OWN STAGE WHEN THEY WON'T GIVE YOU THE MIC

When the world won't listen, turn up your own volume.
Cathy Hughes.

Thirty-two banks said no.

Cathy Hughes needed a loan to buy a radio station. She had a vision, to create programming for the Black community that mainstream radio ignored. Bank after bank rejected her, a Black woman asking for money in the **1970s**.

She had no money left. Her marriage was ending. She was living in the radio station with her young son, bathing him in the bathroom sink.

Most people would have quit after rejection five, after rejection ten, after rejection twenty. Cathy went to **33** banks. Bank thirty-three said yes.

That one yes became WOL AM in Washington, D.C., then more stations, then Radio One, a media empire that went public and made Cathy Hughes a billionaire.

But here is what matters. Cathy did not get lucky on bank thirty-three. She got prepared. Each rejection taught her something, what bankers cared about, what numbers mattered, how to pitch better. By rejection thirty-two, she was not making the same pitch she made at rejection one.

She refused to go off air. She kept broadcasting, kept serving, and kept believing her voice mattered.

This is how relentless persistence, sharpened by adaptation, builds empires.

Reader's Transition

Some people spend their whole lives waiting for someone to hand them a microphone. They knock on doors, send applications, and hope someone will notice them, pick them, and give them a chance to speak.

Smart underdogs don't wait. They build their own stage. You don't beg for a platform. You don't shrink to fit rooms that can't hear you. You build your own room, install your own speakers, and turn up your own volume.

Because when the world tells you to be quiet, that's exactly when you need to get louder.

Building through rejection proves doubters wrong across every industry. Cathy heard "no" from 32 banks, but the principle applies everywhere. In tech, it's 50 VCs passing on your startup before you bootstrap to profitability. In creative fields, it's 100 agents rejecting your manuscript before you self-publish to bestseller status. In education, it's 20 districts rejecting your program before you launch it independently and prove the model works.

As you read Cathy's story, ask yourself: If I knew that "yes" was waiting at rejection #33, how would that change my response to the "no" I just received?

Origin

1947. Omaha, Nebraska.

Catherine Elizabeth Woods is born in the Logan Fontenelle Housing Projects, the projects, the place where people with no money and no options live. Her father is special. William Alfred Woods is the first African American to earn an accounting degree from Creighton University. Her mother, Helen, plays trombone with the International Sweethearts of Rhythm, an all women jazz band.

But degrees and talent do not always mean money. Cathy grows up poor, really poor. At 14, she lies about her age to get a job, not for spending money but to help her family eat. At 16, she gets pregnant. Her mother kicks her out just like that, out of the house, on her own, a teenage girl with a baby on the way and nowhere to go.

Most people would see this as the end. Cathy sees it as fuel. She makes a promise to herself. My son will not become a negative statistic. I will not let poverty win.

She takes classes at the University of Nebraska and at Creighton in business administration. She does not finish because she cannot afford to, but she learns enough. And she discovers something. She loves radio.

As a kid, she was fascinated by it, voices coming through speakers, stories, music, connection. Radio felt like magic. At 19, she gets a job at the Omaha Star, a Black owned newspaper. She sees how Black media serves the community, tells stories mainstream media ignores, and gives voice to people who do not get heard anywhere else.

That understanding changes everything.

In 1969, she gets her first radio job at KOWH, a Black owned station in Omaha. She is hooked. This is what she is meant to do. In 1971, she moves to Washington, D.C., and takes a job as an administrative assistant at Howard University's School of Communications. It is a low level entry position, but it is a foot in the door.

She works at WHUR FM, Howards radio station. She is good, really good. By 1973, she is General Sales Manager. By 1975, she is Vice President and General Manager, the first woman to hold that position at WHUR.

But she does not want to work for someone else forever. She wants to own her own station, build her own platform, and control her own voice. That is when the real battle begins.

Play by Play

1979. Washington, D.C.

Cathy walks into a bank with a business plan, a vision, and a station she wants to buy: WOL-AM. It's a struggling station losing money, but it serves a Black audience. And Cathy knows that audience is valuable, loyal, and powerful.

The banker looks at her paperwork, looks at her, and says no. She tries another bank. No. Another. No.

She's a Black woman asking for money in an industry run by white men. Every banker sees the same thing: high risk, no collateral, bad bet. She keeps going—bank five, bank ten, bank fifteen. No, no, no.

Some bankers ask her about her family plans, when she's having more kids, whether she'll be able to focus on business. They never ask men those questions. No, no, no.

Bank twenty, bank twenty-five, bank thirty. Most people quit after three rejections, maybe five. Cathy is at thirty. Bank thirty-one. No. Bank thirty-two. No.

She walks out of that thirty-second bank empty-handed again—tired, broke, running out of options. But she doesn't stop.

Bank thirty-three.

The banker looks at her plan, thinks, and considers. Finally: "Yes. But the terms are tough." High interest, personal liability, everything she owns is on the line. If this fails, she loses it all.

Cathy takes the deal. She buys WOL-AM in 1980. Finally, her own station. And then everything gets harder.

The breaking point.

The station is bleeding money. Advertisers don't believe Black audiences are profitable. Revenue is terrible, expenses are high. Her second marriage collapses under the stress, and her husband wants out. She has to buy him out of the business—more debt, more pressure.

She's days away from losing everything—the station, the dream, her future. So Cathy does what underdogs do when their backs are against the wall. She moves in. Literally. She and her young son Alfred move into the radio station. They sleep on the floor, use the station bathroom, and eat cheap meals between broadcasts. She calls it "camping out." Her son calls it survival.

She can't afford to hire a full staff, so she does it all herself—morning show host, sales manager, janitor, everything. She works eighteen-hour days, then twenty, then around the clock. She's on air, then off air selling ads, then back on air, then fixing equipment, then back on air again.

Most people would see this as rock bottom. Cathy sees it as leverage. Because she's not just keeping a station running. She's building something bigger.

Breakthrough

The flip.

Cathy flips the stations format, gospel music, R and B, community talk shows. She does not follow what other stations do. She follows what her community needs. She talks about education, employment, and justice, issues that matter to real people living real lives.

She does not chase big ratings. She chases real connection. And slowly, it works.

Advertisers start paying attention, not because the audience is huge but because the audience is loyal. When Cathy speaks, people listen. When people listen, they act. When they act, advertisers pay.

One station becomes profitable. Then she buys a second, then more. The stations become Radio One, a network. Then she adds TV One with television programming for Black audiences. The company becomes Urban One, a media empire.

1999.

Radio One goes public on the stock exchange. Cathy Hughes becomes the first African American woman to chair a publicly traded corporation.

From sleeping on the floor of a failing station to running a multibillion dollar media empire. From thirty-two rejections to making history. From the housing projects to the stock exchange.

That is not luck. That is what happens when you refuse to go off air.

Power Moves

1. Every "no" is training, not a dead end

Cathy didn't get lucky on bank thirty-three. She got prepared. Each rejection taught her something—what bankers care about, what language works, what numbers matter, how to pitch better. By rejection thirty-two, she wasn't making the same pitch she made at rejection one. She was sharper, smarter, and ready.

When you hear "no," don't just walk away sad. Ask: What can I learn? What can I improve? What's missing? Then adjust and try again. Each no trains you for the yes that's coming.

2. Build the platform that's missing

Mainstream radio ignored Black audiences. Cathy didn't beg them to pay attention—she just built her own platform. When you serve a community that's been overlooked, that community doesn't just buy from you. They root for you, tell their friends, and grow with you. Because you're not just selling them something. You're seeing them and giving them space that didn't exist before.

Find the voice that's missing, the community that's ignored, the platform that should exist but doesn't. Then build it—not perfectly, just honestly.

3. Lead with purpose, profit follows

Cathy didn't build Radio One to get rich. She built it to serve her community, to amplify Black voices, to create opportunity. The profit came later as a result, as proof the mission worked.

When your purpose is clear, your message is powerful. People feel the authenticity and trust the intention. And trust builds everything—loyalty, community, legacy. Money follows mission, not always fast, not always easy, but always eventually.

4. Refuse to go off air

Cathy could have quit after rejection five, after rejection twenty, after her marriage ended, after she ran out of money. She didn't. She kept broadcasting, kept serving, and kept believing her voice mattered.

Persistence isn't a personality trait. It's a choice—a choice you make every day when it's hard. Stamina isn't about being tough. It's about being clear. Clear on why you're doing this, who you're serving, and why this matters more than comfort. That clarity keeps you going when everything says quit.

Mind Trap

The Silence Mind Trap: Why rejection makes us shrink instead of grow

Here is what happens when people face rejection. They start to doubt themselves, their voice, and their worth. They think, maybe they are right, maybe I am not ready, maybe I should wait, maybe I should be quieter.

So they shrink. They soften their pitch, lower their voice, and make themselves smaller, hoping that will make people say yes. It does not work. It never works.

Why does this happen. Your brain is designed to keep you safe. And for thousands of years, being rejected from the group meant death. If the tribe kicked you out, you did not survive. So rejection triggers a panic response, and your brain screams, dangerous, retreat, be smaller, fit in.

That instinct saved your ancestors. But it is killing your dreams. Because in the modern world, rejection does not mean death. It means data, information, feedback, and training. But your brain does not know that. It only knows, rejected means bad, must become more acceptable.

So people start changing themselves. They water down their ideas, hide their edge, and try to become what they think others want. And in doing so, they lose the very thing that made them worth listening to.

Here is the truth. The thing that gets you rejected is often the thing that will make you successful.

Cathy's pitch was rejected thirty-two times because it was bold, risky, and different. She wanted to serve a market that banks believed was worthless. If she had changed her pitch to be safer, if she had aimed for mainstream audiences, banks might have said yes sooner. But then she would have built something ordinary, something that already existed, something that did not matter.

The rejection was not a sign she was wrong. It was a sign she was onto something new.

The fix is hard but necessary: When you get rejected, don't shrink. Grow. Don't make yourself smaller. Make your vision clearer. Don't lower your voice. Turn up the volume.

Ask yourself: Am I being rejected because I'm wrong? Or because I'm ahead? If you're wrong, learn and adjust. If you're ahead, keep going.

Cathy didn't change her mission after thirty-two rejections. She sharpened it, clarified it, and got better at explaining it. But she never made it smaller, never made it safer, and never made it less true. And on bank thirty-three, someone finally saw what she saw.

The world doesn't need you to be quieter. It needs you to be clearer, bolder, and more you. Rejection is proof you're trying something new. And new always gets rejected first. Until it doesn't.

Modern Reflection

The old model was simple: wait for traditional gatekeepers to give you access—a record deal, a book deal, a radio show, a platform. If they didn't pick you, you stayed silent. That model is dead.

We live in the platform economy now. Everyone can build their own stage. You don't need a radio station anymore. You have podcasts, YouTube, TikTok, Substack, Twitter, Instagram, and LinkedIn. These are your radio stations, your TV networks, your publishing houses.

Cathy faced thirty-two rejections because banks controlled access to platforms. Today? You can launch a platform in an afternoon for free. The barrier isn't access anymore. It's courage—the courage to post, to publish, to speak, to show up consistently even when the audience is small.

Cathy slept on a radio station floor to keep broadcasting. You can broadcast from your phone on your lunch break. The tools are easier, but the game is the same: serve a community, show up consistently, turn up your volume, and refuse to go off air.

Building in public is the modern version of what Cathy did. She didn't hide behind a corporate brand. She was the voice, the face, the leader. People knew her, trusted her, and connected with her. That's what creators do now—they share their process, their struggles, and their learning. They build community by being real.

And here's what's powerful: You can test faster now. Cathy needed thirty-three banks and months of rejection to get one yes. You can test your idea with thirty-three posts this month. See what resonates, what connects, what people respond to. Then do more of that.

The platforms are there. The audience is waiting. The question is: Will you use your voice?

Because here's what hasn't changed: the world still tries to silence certain voices, women, people of color, people without traditional credentials, people from the "wrong" backgrounds. The difference now? You don't need their permission to speak.

Cathy built Radio One because mainstream radio wouldn't serve Black audiences. Today, you can build your audience directly—no middleman, no gatekeeper, no thirty-two rejections before you get a yes. Just you, your voice, and the people who need to hear it.

The platform is yours to build. The microphone is yours to grab. The volume is yours to control. So stop waiting. Start broadcasting.

Cathy Hughes refused to go off air. Thirty-two rejections, living in a radio station, bathing her son in a bathroom sink—she kept going. That relentless persistence built Radio One, built a billion-dollar media empire, and built a legacy.

Her lesson is powerful: when doors stay closed, build your own building. When everyone says no, keep going until someone says yes.

But here's something that sounds like the opposite—and it's just as true: Sometimes your strongest move is stopping. Not quitting. Not giving up. But choosing to step back, to set a boundary, to say, "I've mastered this, and now I'm protecting something more valuable than medals."

This might seem like a contradiction. Cathy never stopped. Simone chose to stop. But they're not opposites. They're different tools for different moments.

Cathy's moment required building through rejection. Simone's moment required stopping despite expectation.

Both are power moves. The question isn't which one is right. The question is: what does this moment require?

Simone Biles answered that question on the world's biggest stage. And in doing so, she changed what's possible for every athlete who comes after her.

This is what mastery looks like—and why knowing when to walk away is the ultimate form of power.

Part IV
LEGACY MODE

The real win is what you build for others.

You started before you were ready, and you stayed when it got hard. You also built proof until the evidence of your effort spoke louder than any title, and when the world did not open its doors, you built your own.

Now comes the final shift, turning what you have built into something that lasts.

Legacy is not about fame or followers. It is about flow. It is what happens when your courage outlives your circumstances, when what you started continues to create opportunities for others long after you have moved on. The people who make the biggest impact do not chase legacy. They create systems that sustain it, document what they learn, and share what they know. They mentor others quietly, deliberately, and with care because they understand that the true measure of success is not how high you climb, but how many people you lift while you are up there.

Legacy is not built from spotlight moments. It is built from consistency, the small, steady acts that compound over time. It is the manager who makes space for a new voice, the founder who creates access where there was none, or the creator who opens a door and refuses to let it close behind them. That is how movements begin, not with applause, but with continuation.

You did not start this journey to prove anyone wrong. You started to prove what is possible, and in doing so, you became the example someone else will point to when they are told they are not ready, not qualified, or not enough.

This final part of the book is about that, how to protect your progress, share your knowledge, and lead in a way that multiplies opportunity. It is about designing your impact as intentionally as you designed your door. Because someday, someone will walk through the space you created, and for them, it will not feel like a fight, it will feel like a possibility.

That is legacy.

You started without permission. Now help someone else do the same.

Build forward. Leave proof. Create pathways.

The movement doesn't end here — it continues through you.

CHAPTER 10

MASTER THE RULES BEFORE YOU REWRITE THEM

> *Learn the game so well that you earn the right to change it.*
> **Simone Biles.**

Simone Biles is the greatest gymnast of all time. Seven Olympic medals, twenty-five World Championship medals, and moves named after her that no one else can do.

In Tokyo 2021, the world watched as she walked away from competition. She chose safety over medals, selfcare over expectations, and her humanity over her legacy. And that choice—stepping back from the Olympics— might be the most powerful thing she ever did.

It changed sports culture overnight. Athletes everywhere started talking about mental health, about boundaries, about being human first and performer second.

But Simone earned that power long before Tokyo. She didn't just learn gymnastics skills. She learned how the sport works—how judges score, what coaches value, how organizations operate. She studied the whole system, the official rules and the unofficial ones.

She mastered traditional skills before inventing new ones. Proved she could execute perfectly within the current system before pushing past it. That mastery gave her credibility. When she spoke about abuse in USA

Gymnastics, people listened. When she testified before Congress, they heard her. When she withdrew in Tokyo, they respected her choice.

This is how you master a system well enough to reform it—and why knowing when to stop is the ultimate power move.

Reader's Transition

Some people break rules because they are rebellious. They want attention, want to feel special, want to prove they are different. That is not power. That is noise.

Smart underdogs break rules differently. They master the rules first, learn every detail, every standard, every expectation. Then they earn the credibility to rewrite them.

You cannot change a system you do not understand. You cannot improve what you have not mastered. When you walk into a space, you have two paths. You can fight the system from the outside, complain about it, criticize it, demand it change. Or you can learn it from the inside, master it, excel within it, then use that credibility to evolve it.

One gets you ignored. The other gets you heard. Because when someone who has mastered the system says this needs to change, people listen. When someone who has never played the game says it, people dismiss them.

Master the craft. Then unleash the creativity. Learn the politics. Then change the play. Respect the system. Then redefine the standard. That is how underdogs change the world.

This sequence creates credibility across every industry. Simone mastered gymnastics before changing it, but the principle applies everywhere. In tech, it is becoming a senior engineer before proposing better development processes. In healthcare, it is excelling in clinical care before advocating for systemic reforms. In corporate environments, it is delivering results and getting promoted before pushing for cultural changes.

As you read Simone's story, ask yourself, am I skilled enough in my field that when I propose improvements, people listen, and if not, what mastery do I still need to build.

Origin

Columbus, Ohio.

Simone Biles is born into chaos. Her mother, Shannon, struggles with alcoholism and drug addiction. Her birth father abandons the family. Shannon can't take care of Simone and her three siblings. The state steps in—foster care. Simone is too young to understand what's happening, just that home isn't safe, that she and her siblings are being moved around, that nothing is stable.

She's three years old when her grandfather shows up. Ron Biles, Shannon's father, an Air Force veteran and former air traffic controller. He and his wife Nellie have been watching this disaster unfold and make a decision: Ron and Nellie adopt Simone and her younger sister Adria. Simone's older brother and sister go to live with Ron's sister. The family splits, but at least the younger girls have a chance now.

Ron and Nellie move them to Spring, Texas, a suburb of Houston. Nellie is a trained nurse who owns nursing homes. They have stability, structure, and safety. For the first time in her life, Simone has a real home. She starts calling Ron and Nellie "Mom" and "Dad" because that's what they are.

But Simone isn't an easy kid. She's full of energy, constantly moving, running, jumping, and climbing on everything. She describes herself as "a very brave child"—maybe too brave. She doesn't think before she jumps. She just jumps.

School is hard. She can't sit still, can't focus. Teachers complain, other kids get frustrated with her. At age six, she gets diagnosed with ADHD—attention-deficit/hyperactivity disorder. The doctors prescribe Ritalin, a stimulant that helps her focus. It works. She can concentrate better, complete tasks, and follow instructions. But all that energy has to go somewhere.

The discovery.

One day, her daycare takes the kids on a field trip to a gymnastics gym. Simone watches older girls practicing—teenagers doing flips, twists, routines on beams and bars. While the other kids watch, Simone starts copying them, just imitating what she sees with no training, no coaching, just raw natural ability.

The coaches stop and stare. This six-year-old is doing what teenagers do—not perfectly, but she's doing it. They write a note to Ron and Nellie: "Your daughter should take gymnastics classes."

Play by Play

Building mastery.

Simone starts training at Bannon's Gymnastix in Houston under Coach Aimee Boorman. The energetic kid who couldn't sit still in school? She's focused now, six to eight hours a day, learning skills, perfecting form, and building strength. Nellie helps too—every year, she sits down with Simone, they write goals for the next twelve months, track progress, and celebrate wins.

At age fourteen, Simone makes a choice. To go elite in gymnastics means sacrifice—no normal teenage life, no hanging out with friends after school, no parties, no distractions. She leaves public school, gets homeschooled, and trains harder.

2011: She competes in her first junior national competition, the American Classic in Houston. Third place all-around, first place vault. She's good, really good.

2012: More competitions, more wins. She makes the Junior National Team, but she's fifteen—a few months too young to try for the 2012 Olympics team. She has to wait.

The breakdown and breakthrough.

2013: She turns senior, competes internationally for the first time, and wins gold medals in Italy and Germany. She's dominating. Then it all falls apart.

At the 2013 U.S. Classic, Simone loses control. She falls off the balance beam, falls during floor exercise. Her coach pulls her from the meet. People start talking: "Is she choking under pressure?" "Does she have what it takes?" "Maybe she's not mentally strong enough."

Simone is devastated. She worked so hard, was supposed to be unstoppable, and now everyone's questioning her. She goes to a sports psychologist, attends a private camp with legendary coach Márta Károlyi. Something clicks. She learns to block out expectations, to stop worrying about what people think, to enjoy the moment instead of fearing failure.

Three weeks later, she wins the USA Gymnastics National Championship. Dominates. First place. Two months after that, she wins the World Championships in Belgium—her first international title.

From that point on, Simone Biles has not lost a meet. Not one.

Pushing boundaries.

She starts pushing boundaries, adding extra flips and twists, doing moves no one else attempts. In 2013, she invents a new floor exercise skill—a double layout with a half-twist. It gets named after her: "The Biles." She invents more on vault and beam. They all get named after her.

The judges don't even know how to score some of her moves—they're too difficult, too risky. But Simone lands them every time.

By 2014, Ron and Nellie open their own gym: World Champions Centre in Spring, Texas, where Aimee Boorman and Simone train. Simone keeps winning—Nationals, World Championships. She's finishing ahead of competitors by whole points, not fractions.

2015: Third consecutive world title. More golds than any female gymnast in history. She's named Team USA Athlete of the Year.

2016: Olympic year.

The year she's been building toward her entire life. At the Rio Olympics, Simone dominates: team gold, all-around gold, vault gold, floor exercise gold, and balance beam bronze (her only mistake). Four gold medals, one bronze. She carries the American flag in the closing ceremony. She's the most decorated American gymnast of all time with nineteen total medals, undefeated since 2013.

But then something happens that changes everything.

Breakthrough

The exposure.

After Rio, Russian hackers leak medical records showing that Simone tested positive for Ritalin. They are trying to discredit her and suggest she cheated. Simone does not hide. She speaks openly and says, I have ADHD, I have taken Ritalin since I was a kid, the Olympics Committee approved it, I am not ashamed. Her honesty helps thousands of kids with ADHD feel less alone.

She takes a year off after Rio, thirteen years of nonstop training and competition. She needs a break.

The reckoning.

Then in January 2018, the gymnastics world explodes. Larry Nassar, Team USA's doctor, is exposed. Over 150 women and girls accuse him of sexual abuse—abuse that happened while he was supposed to be treating them. On January 18, 2018, Simone Biles adds her name to the list. She was abused by the doctor everyone trusted while the organizations that were supposed to protect her did nothing.

Nassar is sentenced to prison for the rest of his life. But the damage is done. Simone struggles with depression. She sleeps constantly to escape, has trouble trusting doctors. The trauma affects everything. But she refuses to let it define her. She goes to therapy and keeps training.

In 2018, she returns to competition. At the USA Gymnastics National Championships, she wins all five gold medals—first woman in history to do that. She wears a teal leotard. Teal is the color of solidarity with sexual assault survivors. She doesn't make a speech. She doesn't need to. The leotard speaks for her.

She keeps competing, keeps winning. At the 2019 World Championships, she becomes the most decorated gymnast in history—male or female, ever. Then COVID-19 hits, and the 2020 Tokyo Olympics are postponed to 2021.

Tokyo: The choice.

When she finally competes in Tokyo, something is wrong. In the middle of a vault routine, Simone loses her sense of space. Gymnasts call it the twisties. She cannot tell where she is in the air, cannot tell when she will land. It is dangerous. If she keeps competing like this, she could break her neck, become paralyzed, or die.

She withdraws from the team competition after one vault. The world watches. Some people support her. Many attack her. They say she is weak, she is a quitter, she let her team down, mental health is just an excuse. The pressure is crushing. She is supposed to be perfect, supposed to be unbreakable, supposed to win no matter what.

But Simone makes a different choice. She prioritizes her safety, her mental health, and her life. She says, I am more than my medals, I am a human being.

On the last day of competition, she returns, competes on balance beam, and wins bronze, her seventh Olympic medal, tying Shannon Miller for the most ever by an American gymnast. But the real win is not the medal. It is the message.

She showed the world that knowing when to stop is strength, not weakness. That protecting yourself matters more than meeting expectations. That you can say no even when everyone is watching. She redefined what it means to be a champion, not only someone who wins but someone who knows their worth beyond the winning.

The legacy.

In 2022, President Biden awards her the Presidential Medal of Freedom, the nation's highest civilian honor. In 2023, at age 26, she returns to competition and wins her eighth national all-around title, breaking a 90-year record. In 2024, at age 27, she competes in Paris: three more golds, one silver. Eleven Olympic medals total, seven gold—the most for any American gymnast ever.

From foster care to the most decorated gymnast in history. From a system that failed to protect her to a champion who protects herself. From mastering every rule to rewriting the most important one: you're more than your performance.

That's not luck. That's what happens when you master the system and then use your credibility to change it.

Power Moves

1. Learn the politics before you change the game

Simone didn't just learn gymnastics skills. She learned how the sport works—how judges score, what coaches value, how the organizations operate, what the media cares about. She studied the whole system, the official rules and the unofficial ones.

That's why when she spoke about abuse, people listened. She wasn't an outsider criticizing. She was an insider who'd won everything, who knew the system better than anyone.

You can't change a power structure you haven't decoded. Study how decisions get made, who has real influence, and what the unwritten rules are. Then use that knowledge to propose better.

2. Master the craft before you break boundaries

Simone spent years perfecting traditional skills before she invented new ones. She learned every basic vault, beam routine, and floor exercise perfectly. Only then did she start adding moves no one had done before.

That mastery gave her credibility. When she did something impossible, judges and coaches didn't dismiss it—they respected it because they knew she'd mastered everything else first.

You earn the right to innovate by proving you can execute excellently within the current system. Master the fundamentals. Then push past them.

3. Use your platform to evolve the system

Simone didn't just complain about USA Gymnastics failing to protect athletes. She used her credibility as the greatest gymnast ever to demand change. She testified, spoke out, wore teal, and withdrew in Tokyo. Every action said: "This system needs to value human beings, not just medals."

She didn't burn it down. She evolved it, used her insider status to push for reform. When you've mastered a system, you earn the right to improve it. Use that right.

4. Know that stopping can be your strongest move

Simone's greatest moment wasn't winning gold. It was walking away from it. In Tokyo, she chose safety over medals, self-care over expectations, and life over legacy. That choice changed sports culture—suddenly, athletes everywhere started talking about mental health, about boundaries, about being human first and performer second.

The highest mastery isn't doing more. It's knowing when enough is enough.

Mind Trap

The Perfectionist Mind Trap: When mastery becomes a prison

Here is what happens when you commit to mastering something. You get really good at it, people expect excellence from you, and you start expecting it from yourself. At first, it feels good, you are disciplined, focused, and committed. Then the pressure builds. You cannot make mistakes, cannot have off days, cannot be human. The mastery that gave you freedom becomes a cage.

Simone felt this in Tokyo. She had mastered gymnastics so completely that the world expected perfection every time, with no exceptions. When she got the twisties, she could not simply say she was struggling, because she was Simone Biles, the greatest ever. She was not allowed to struggle.

Why does this happen. Because your brain confuses your worth with your performance. It tells you that if you are not perfect, you are nothing. The higher you climb; the more pressure you feel. The more you achieve, the less room you have to be human.

You start thinking, I cannot stop now, I cannot show weakness, I cannot let people down. So you push through pain, through fear, through exhaustion, through warning signs that say stop. And sometimes, you break.

Here is the truth. Mastery is about discipline, not perfection. Discipline means showing up consistently, doing the work, learning from mistakes, and growing over time. Perfection means never making mistakes, never struggling, never being human. One is sustainable. The other is impossible.

Simone reached a level of mastery where people forgot she was human, where one fall or one mistake became international news, where she was not allowed to have limits. The mental trap is believing that mastery means you cannot stop, cannot rest, cannot choose yourself over the performance.

The fix is remembering why you started. You did not master this thing to become a machine. You mastered it because you loved it, because it challenged you, because it made you feel alive. When mastery stops feeling like growth and starts feeling like a prison, that is the signal, not to quit forever, but to pause, to reset, to remember you are a person first and a performer second.

Simone did not quit gymnastics in Tokyo. She paused, protected herself, and then came back when she was ready on her terms, not anyone else's. That is the difference between healthy mastery and the perfectionist trap. Healthy mastery leaves room for being human. The trap demands that you sacrifice your humanity for the performance.

Do not fall for it. Master the craft, but do not let the craft master you. Know when to push. And know when to stop. Both are strength.

Modern Reflection

The old rule in sports was simple: push through everything—pain, fear, injury, trauma, mental struggle. Athletes who stopped for any reason were called weak, quitters, failures. That rule is finally changing. And Simone Biles is a big reason why.

Mental health is no longer taboo in sports or work. When Simone withdrew in Tokyo, the conversation shifted. Athletes started speaking openly about anxiety, depression, burnout, and trauma—tennis player Naomi Osaka, swimmer Michael Phelps, NBA player Kevin Love. They all said: "We're human beings, not performance machines."

That honesty is spreading beyond sports into workplaces, schools, and families. People are finally saying: "I need help. I'm struggling. I can't do this right now." And instead of being punished, they're being supported. Simone helped create that shift by being the best and still choosing herself.

The "always hustle" culture is being questioned. For years, the message was: work harder, sleep less, never stop, never quit. Burnout was a badge of honor. Rest was for the weak. That's changing. People are realizing that sustainable excellence requires rest, boundaries, and mental health care.

You can't perform at your best when you're running on empty. You can't innovate when you're exhausted. You can't lead when you're breaking. The most productive people aren't the ones who never stop—they're the ones who know when to stop and recharge.

Mastery plus humanity is the new standard. The old model was: be excellent at any cost, sacrifice everything—your health, your relationships, your sanity. The new model is: be excellent AND take care of yourself, master your craft AND maintain your boundaries, achieve greatness AND stay human.

That's what Simone showed us. You don't have to choose between being the best and being healthy. You can be both. In fact, being healthy is what lets you stay the best for longer.

Here's what this means for you in 2025 and beyond: You don't have to burn yourself out to prove you're committed. You don't have to sacrifice your mental health to achieve success. You don't have to push through everything to be taken seriously.

Master your craft—yes. Work hard—yes. Be disciplined—yes. But also: rest, set boundaries, ask for help, and choose yourself when you need to. That's not weakness. That's wisdom.

Simone mastered gymnastics more than anyone in history. She also mastered something even harder: knowing when to stop. Both skills matter. Both are strength.

Simone Biles mastered gymnastics so completely that she earned the right to reform it from the inside. She learned the system, dominated the system, and then used her credibility to demand that the system protect athletes, not exploit them. Her withdrawal in Tokyo was not weakness. It was power, the power that comes from mastery.

But Simone's path, mastering a system to change it, is not the only path. Sometimes you do not need to master the old system. Sometimes you build a new one so undeniably successful that the old system becomes irrelevant.

That is what Olamide Olowe did. One hundred investors told her there was no market for her skin care brand, that people like her were not profitable, that she should give up. She did not try to convince them. She did not master their system to earn their respect.

She simply built, publicly, loudly, undeniably. She used every lesson we have covered. She started before she was ready, as in Chapter 1, Issa. She stacked small wins into proof, as in Chapter 7, Viola. She tracked every metric, as in Chapter 8, Janice. She built despite rejection, as in Chapter 9, Cathy.

And she added one more element. She built so publicly that her success created F O M O in the very investors who rejected her.

This is the culmination. When you build proof so comprehensive, so visible, so undeniable that rejection becomes your competitive advantage.

This is how you turn no into leverage.

CHAPTER 11

BUILD RECEIPTS THAT SILENCE DOUBT

When you have proof, you don't need permission.
Olamide Olowe.

One hundred investors were not convinced.

Olamide Olowe was a young Black woman pitching a skin care brand for people with hyperpigmentation. Investors told her there was no market, no demand, and no future. She could have believed them.

Instead, she built Topicals anyway, publicly, loudly, undeniably. She documented everything, customer testimonials, clinical results, before and after photos, sales data. She shared wins on social media, posted behind the scenes content, and built a waitlist of **13000** people before launch.

When she finally launched at Sephora, Topicals became the fastest growing brand they had ever seen. Products sold out in hours, TikTok videos went viral, and press coverage exploded. And some of those investors who said no came back, asking if it was too late to invest.

That is the power of building proof so comprehensive that rejection becomes leverage. Olamide did not convince skeptics with better pitches. She built results so strong they created F O M O, fear of missing out. Investors who passed early watched her succeed without them.

This is the culmination of everything, start before you are ready, as in Chapter 1, stack small wins, as in Chapter 7, track your value, as in Chapter 8, persist through rejection, as in Chapter 9, and build so publicly and undeniably that the market comes to you.

This is how rejection becomes your competitive advantage.

Reader's Transition

Some people fight bias with anger, with arguments, and with demands to be taken seriously. They explain themselves, defend themselves, and try to convince skeptics that they are wrong. That is exhausting, and it rarely works.

Smart underdogs fight differently. They fight with evidence, with data, and with results so clear that doubt becomes irrelevant. When stereotypes say you cannot, receipts say you already did. When bias questions your worth, proof answers without speaking. When doubt tries to silence you, documentation makes you undeniable.

You do not need the loudest voice. You need the clearest evidence. Track every win, save every testimonial, and document every result. When you walk into a room with receipts, three things happen. Arguments end before they start, because evidence speaks louder than assumptions. Bias loses power, because facts are objective and cannot be dismissed like opinions. Your confidence grows, because when you see your own proof, you stop questioning yourself.

You do not need to convince everyone. You only need to show what is true. Truth is difficult to argue with.

Public proof creates F O M O across every industry. Olamide faced **100** investor rejections in beauty, but the principle applies everywhere. In tech, it means building to **50000** users so that venture capital groups who passed come back wanting to invest. In creative fields, it means growing to **100000** followers so that agents who rejected you now pursue you. In consulting, it means building such strong client results that firms that refused to hire you now want to acquire you.

As you read Olamide's story, ask yourself, how could I build my results so publicly and so undeniably that rejection becomes the rejectors' loss, not mine?

Origin

October 27, 1997. United States.

Olamide Olowe is born to Nigerian immigrant parents, first generation Nigerian American. Her father is a doctor, and for a time, her family builds and runs their own medical clinics. Young Olamide grows up believing she will follow in his footsteps, become a doctor, and help people.

But she also grows up with something painful, chronic skin conditions, hyperpigmentation, post barbae folliculitis, inflammation, and dark spots. She tries everything, products from the pharmacy, home remedies, but nothing works quite right. She feels embarrassed, different, and wrong.

She starts mixing her own ingredients in the kitchen, experimenting, trying to create something that helps, something that works for skin like hers. She watches early beauty content on YouTube, learns, tests, and adjusts. But the shame does not go away, the feeling of being different, of having "problem skin".

El Paso, Texas. High school.

Olamide attends El Dorado High School, then Faith Christian High School. She's a track star, really good, and sets her school's record in the 400m race while winning regional meets. In 2012, she finishes second in the 200m at the USATF Region 10 Junior Olympic Track Championships. As a freshman, she wins state championships in long jump, 100 meters, and the 4x100-meter relay. She's talented, dedicated, and fast.

UCLA offers her a full-ride scholarship for track and field—Division I athlete. She takes it.

2015-2019. UCLA.

Olamide enrolls as a pre-med student with the plan to become a dermatologist and help people with skin like hers, fixing the problem from inside the medical system. But balancing pre-med coursework with Division I track is brutal, exhausting, and overwhelming.

Her roommate introduces her to Rechelle Dennis, daughter of Richelieu Dennis, the founder of SheaMoisture. This connection changes everything. Olamide co-founds SheaGIRL, a subsidiary brand of SheaMoisture, while still in college and still running track. She loves it—the business side, the creative side, the impact side.

She starts thinking: maybe I don't need to be a dermatologist to change skincare. Maybe I can do it as an entrepreneur instead. She graduates from UCLA in 2019 with a degree in Political Science and Entrepreneurship. But she's not done yet. She has another idea, a bigger idea.

The parallel path.

1997: Claudia Teng is born, Asian American, and grows up with severe eczema. It's bad, really bad. She hides her topical steroid creams so people won't ask questions, feels isolated, embarrassed, and ashamed.

In high school, she starts working as a dermatology clinical research assistant and sees the healthcare system up close. She notices something disturbing: clinical trials lack representation for people of color, treatments are rarely tested on darker skin tones, and the effectiveness on diverse skin is understudied.

She goes to UC Berkeley, studies Gender and Women's Studies while pursuing pre-med, conducts dermatology research, and authors peer-reviewed articles about skin cancers and rare genetic diseases like Epidermolysis Bullosa. She's planning to go to medical school, become a dermatologist, and change the system from inside. But something's missing—the medical world feels too slow, too clinical, too removed from the real people suffering.

Play by Play

2019. Los Angeles.

Olamide and Claudia meet through a mutual friend. They start talking, sharing stories, and realize they lived the same experience. Both had chronic skin conditions as kids, both felt ashamed, both hid their treatments, both were premed students planning to become dermatologists, and both were frustrated with the beauty industry's perfect skin obsession.

They see the same gap, the same problem, the same opportunity. The standard beauty industry does not serve people with chronic skin issues. Products are clinical, sterile, white packaging, pharmacy aisles. Everything about it says, you are broken, you need fixing. And people of color are especially underserved. Most products are not tested on darker skin tones, do not address hyperpigmentation, and do not understand the specific challenges.

Olamide and Claudia decide they are not going to medical school. They are going to build the brand that should exist.

2018-2020. The grind.

They start working on Topicals around 2018, developing products, testing formulas, and building a brand. They need money, so they start pitching investors. Over the next two years, they pitch over 100 investors, and the rejections pile up over and over.

One investor tells Olamide her name is "weird" and just dismisses her. Another investor calls their market "dormant demand" and says chronic skin conditions are too taboo, can't prove a market exists. Multiple investors say the beauty market is oversaturated: "Nothing new here."

They spend their last dollars traveling to pitch meetings, running out of money, options, and hope.

Early 2020.

Finally, they plan to launch in March 2020. Then COVID-19 hits, the pandemic shuts everything down, supply chains collapse, and the launch gets delayed. They reschedule for summer 2020. Then George Floyd is murdered, social unrest erupts, and Olamide and Claudia choose to delay again, focusing their energy on supporting the Black Lives Matter movement instead. They're exhausted, broke, and delayed twice. But they keep going.

The turning point.

An unnamed female investor—someone who backed Glossier and Warby Parker early—sees their vision and believes in them. She writes a $2 million check. That changes everything. Other investors follow: Lerer Hippeau leads, Mucker Capital joins, and high-profile Black women invest including Netflix CMO Bozoma Saint John, Issa Rae, Yvonne Orji, and DJ Hannah Bronfman.

By August 2020, they've raised $2.6 million in seed funding.

August 2020. Launch.

Topicals officially launches with two products: "Like Butter" (a hydrating face mask for dry, sensitive, and eczema-prone skin) and "Faded" (a brightening serum for hyperpigmentation and dark spots).

They're not just selling products—they're selling a philosophy: "Funner Flare-ups," reframing skin conditions not as flaws to fix but as part of identity to care for with pride. The packaging is colorful, vibrant, and fun—the opposite of sterile pharmacy products. The messaging is honest, mental health-aware, and community-focused.

They'd built a waitlist of over 13,000 people before launch through social media. The anticipation is huge. The products sell out at Nordstrom and on their website within days.

Breakthrough

The power of proof.

But the real breakthrough comes from how they built their proof. Topicals doesn't buy traditional ads—they build community. They encourage user-generated content: real customers posting before-and-after videos, raw, unfiltered, and honest. People with hyperpigmentation showing how "Faded" actually works, people with eczema showing how "Like Butter" soothes their skin.

The videos go viral, not because they're polished but because they're real. Topicals reposts customer content, makes "marginalized skincare stories into main character content," and celebrates real skin, real results, and real people. They work with authentic influencers—not the biggest, but the most aligned—BIPOC creators who genuinely understand the mission. They use humor and memes, creating "skin talk" that's informative and entertaining.

The brand's message—"embrace your skin, flare-ups and all"—resonates with Gen Z, with people tired of "perfect skin" standards. It becomes a cultural moment, not just a trend.

March 2021. Sephora.

Just seven months after launch, Topicals appears on Sephora.com. It is more than a retail deal. They are selected for the Sephora Accelerate program, an incubator for BIPOC owned beauty brands that provides mentorship, business training, resources, and a curriculum created specifically to support success at Sephora.

Olamide and Claudia do not pitch potential. They pitch proof. They present metrics, social proof, their 13,000-person waitlist, their TikTok virality, and their sell out launches. Their message is clear: we already have demand, we already have community, we already have results.

Sephora says yes. The first shipment of Topicals products at Sephora sells out in less than 48 hours.

2022.

Topicals becomes the fastest-growing skincare brand at Sephora in the United States, selling a product every minute. In November 2022, they raise $10 million in Series A funding led by CAVU Consumer Partners. Jay-Z's Marcy Venture Partners invests, Gabrielle Union invests, and Kelly Rowland invests.

At age 25, Olamide Olowe becomes the youngest Black woman ever to raise $10 million in a single funding round. She broke her own record from 2020 when she became the youngest Black woman to raise $2 million.

2024.

They raise another $10 million in another Series A round with CAVU leading again. Total raised: $25 million.

Topicals expands to Sephora UK. Olamide and Topicals President Sochi Mbadugha launch a holding company: Cost of Doing Business (CODB) with a mission to acquire and build businesses that prioritize culture and community.

April 2025.

CODB acquires Bread Beauty Supply, a hair care brand. Olamide is 27 years old—CEO of Topicals, founder of CODB, an investor, and an entrepreneur.

From the girl who hid her skin condition to the CEO building a beauty empire for people like her. From 100+ investor rejections to $25 million raised. From "dormant demand" to fastest-growing brand at Sephora. From shame to pride, from hiding to building, from doubt to receipts.

That's not luck. That's what happens when you document every win and let proof speak.

Power Moves

1. Track every win as it happens

Olamide and Claudia did not wait until they were successful to start tracking. They documented from day one. Customer testimonials, before and after photos, sales data, engagement metrics, and clinical results. When investors said "prove there is demand," they had a 13,000-person waitlist. When Sephora asked "can you scale?" they had viral TikTok proof and sellout launches.

You cannot prove your value six months from now if you do not track it today. Start now. Every win, every result, every piece of feedback. Save it. Document it.

2. Keep receipts that prove your value

Olamide walked into pitch meetings with portfolios, not just ideas but proof: customer reviews, clinical data, sales numbers, viral videos, and press coverage. She didn't ask investors to trust her vision—she showed them evidence the vision was already working.

Receipts beat bias. When you have data, stereotypes can't touch you. Every positive email, every completed project, every metric that improved—save it, file it, and keep it ready.

3. Share your wins publicly and consistently

Topicals didn't succeed in private then announce it—they built in public. They shared customer stories, celebrated wins, posted behind-the-scenes content, and documented the journey. That visibility created momentum—more customers, more press, more investors.

When you share consistently, you build a track record people can see. Your success becomes undeniable because it's documented and public.

4. Let results silence doubt

After 100+ rejections, Olamide didn't convince the skeptics—she built results so strong they became irrelevant. Products that sold out, a waitlist of 13,000, viral TikTok content, and the fastest-growing brand at Sephora. The proof made the arguments unnecessary. Investors who said no early now watched her succeed without them.

You don't need to convince everyone. Just build results clear enough that doubt looks foolish.

Mind Trap

The Invisibility Mind Trap: Why we don't document our wins

Here's what stops most people from keeping receipts. They think: "My wins aren't that impressive. Who cares about this small success? I don't want to seem arrogant." So they do good work, create value, and get results, then move on without documenting any of it.

Six months later, someone asks "what have you accomplished?" and they blank. They have no receipts, no proof, no documented track record. They worked hard, but nobody knows it—including them.

Why does this happen? Because of imposter syndrome—even when you succeed, your brain says: "That wasn't really me. That was luck. That's not worth documenting." Or false humility—the idea that "my work should speak for itself. I shouldn't have to brag." Or perfectionism—"This isn't good enough to save yet. I'll document it when I do something really impressive."

But here's the truth: Invisible work doesn't count. If it's not documented, it didn't happen—not because it's not real, but because nobody can see it, nobody can reference it, and nobody can pay you for it.

Olamide faced 100+ rejections partly because early investors couldn't see proof of demand. But once she had receipts—waitlist numbers, early sales data, customer testimonials—investors couldn't say no as easily. The work was always good, but proof made it undeniable.

The fix is changing your relationship with documentation: Documenting wins isn't bragging—it's recordkeeping, protecting your value, and building leverage for future negotiations.

Every week, spend five minutes saving receipts: screenshot positive feedback, save "thank you" emails, record project outcomes with numbers, collect customer testimonials, and note problems solved and impact created. This isn't arrogance. This is survival.

Because in a world that underestimates underdogs, receipts are your defense. When bias questions your worth, data answers. When stereotypes say you can't, your track record says you already did.

Stop hiding your wins. Start saving them. Because the work you don't document is work you can't prove. And work you can't prove? Nobody pays you for.

Modern Reflection

When Olamide and Claudia launched Topicals in 2020, they didn't have traditional marketing budgets. They couldn't afford TV ads or celebrity endorsements. So they built in public on TikTok, on Instagram, through user-generated content.

Now, in 2025, building in public isn't just a strategy. It's the strategy.

Social proof is the new resume. Your LinkedIn shows your job history, but your TikTok shows your work in action, your Instagram shows your results, and your YouTube shows your process. Employers, clients, and investors don't just want to know where you worked—they want to see what you built, what you created, and what results you delivered. Building in public means real-time receipts.

Content creation is documentation. Every post you share is a receipt—every video demonstrating your work, every article explaining your process, every case study showing your results. You're not just creating content. You're creating proof. Topicals' TikTok strategy wasn't just marketing—it was documentation. Every user-generated video was a receipt proving their products worked.

Portfolio careers require visible proof. The days of working one job for 40 years are over. Most people now have portfolio careers with multiple income streams, freelance work, and side businesses. In that world, your receipts matter more than ever. You need to show what you've done, who you've helped, and what results you've created. Your portfolio isn't just projects. It's proof.

Here's what this means for you: You have more tools than ever to build receipts. Social media for sharing wins publicly, screenshots for saving feedback, cloud storage for organizing proof, video for documenting process, and analytics for tracking metrics. The barrier is not access. It is consistency.

Start now. Document everything. Share your process. Build your proof publicly. Because in 2025 and beyond, your receipts are your resume, your track record is your credibility, and your documented wins are your leverage.

Olamide showed 13,000 people waiting for her product. That is a receipt investors could not ignore. What receipts are you building?

AFTERWORD

A Final Note: The Proof Is You

If you have made it this far, you have already done something most people never do. You have stayed the course.

You have seen what happens when underdogs stop waiting for permission, when they choose action over approval, and when they learn to build proof instead of asking for it.

You have watched each story unfold, and hopefully, you have seen pieces of your own story reflected back.

Now it is your turn.

You do not need a perfect plan, a title, a team, or a greenlight. You just need a decision, one honest and fearless moment when you say, "I am done waiting."

The truth is that no one ever feels ready. Readiness is a story we tell ourselves to delay risk. But movement does not come from readiness. It comes from responsibility. You have something to build, something to say, something to prove.

So start small, stack your wins, build your proof, and create your door. And when you walk through it, hold it open for someone else. That is how momentum becomes legacy. Because in the end, this book is not about them.

It is not even about me. It is about you and what you will build when you stop waiting for the world to notice.

You have already earned your permission. Now go make it undeniable.

Start without permission. The proof is you.

ACKNOWLEDGEMENTS

No book is written alone. Even the ones that begin in quiet moments, the late nights, the drafts no one reads, the doubts no one sees, are shaped by people who show up in small and powerful ways.

To my family, thank you for being my first foundation.

To my mother, who taught me to stay when it was hard and to remember why I started. Your voice has followed me into every room.

To the women whose stories fill these pages, thank you for giving your brilliance, your truth, and your grit to the world. You built proof long before it was recognized. You made space where there was none, and because of that, we all have more room to rise.

To my mentors, colleagues, and friends, thank you for the lessons, the late night talks, and the quiet pushes that reminded me to keep going. Each of you left a fingerprint on this book in ways you may never know.

To the underdogs, the unseen, the uninvited, the unstoppable, thank you for existing as living proof that ambition and authenticity can coexist. Your stories inspired every line of this work.

And finally, to the reader holding this book, thank you for trusting me with your time, your hope, and your belief that something better is possible. My greatest wish is that this book becomes more than words, that it becomes your proof.

You are the reason this book exists.

You are the continuation of its story.

Keep building. Keep showing up.

And never wait for permission.

ABOUT THE AUTHOR

Phoebe A. Bryant is a business professional and writer who has spent her career building a place for herself in rooms where few expected her to belong.

From her start as an IT intern to her rise as a technology business partner, Phoebe's journey embodies what it means to begin without permission. Over the years, she has built programs and led global initiatives that connect people, technology, and purpose, all while championing opportunities for those often overlooked in corporate and creative spaces.

Phoebe is also a scholar-practitioner who holds a doctorate in business. Her approach blends technical expertise with human insight, proving that grit, creativity, and heart can coexist in any field.

She writes, speaks, and mentors on perseverance, the underdog advantage, and building careers without traditional pathways. Her mission is to help others see that readiness is not a requirement. It is a result of starting.

When she is not writing or speaking, Phoebe can be found mentoring emerging professionals, studying the intersection of data security and human behavior, or finding inspiration in the everyday stories of people who build their own doors.

NOTES

Chapter 1

Issa Rae

Biographical information from Wikipedia, s.v. "Issa Rae," last modified October 2024, https://en.wikipedia.org/wiki/Issa_Rae.

"Awkward Black Girl," Wikipedia, last modified July 7, 2025, https://en.wikipedia.org/wiki/Awkward_Black_Girl. The Kickstarter campaign raised $56,269 from 1,960 backers by August 11, 2011.

"How Issa Rae Is Building a Media Conglomerate," Creators Blueprint, October 3, 2022, https://www.creatorsblueprint.co/p/how-issa-rae-is-becoming-a-media. Issa's YouTube channel accumulated more than 25 million views by 2014.

"Insecure—Awards," IMDb, accessed November 2025, https://www.imdb.com/title/tt5024912/awards/.

Issa Rae, *The Misadventures of Awkward Black Girl* (New York: 37 Ink/Atria, 2015).

Post-*Insecure* production work documented in "Hoorae Media," Wikipedia, last modified August 23, 2025, https://en.wikipedia.org/wiki/Hoorae_Media; "'Insecure' Creator Issa Rae Just Signed a Deal to Produce," CNN, March 25, 2021, https://www.cnn.com/2021/03/24/business/issa-rae-warnermedia-deal; "Issa Rae and

Hollywood's Unkept Promises," TIME, February 1, 2024, https://time.com/collection/closers/6564918/issa-rae-hollywoods-unkept-promises/.

Chapter 2

Patrice Banks

Biographical information from Wikipedia, s.v. "Patrice Banks," last modified October 30, 2024, https://en.wikipedia.org/wiki/Patrice_Banks; "Patrice Banks: An Auto Clinic Where Girls Rule," Lehigh University News, accessed November 2025, https://news.lehigh.edu/patrice-banks-an-auto-clinic-where-girls-rule.

"Patrice Banks '02: Empowering Women through Wrenches and Car Lifts," Lehigh University Engineering, June 13, 2019, https://engineering.lehigh.edu/news/article/patrice-banks-02-empowering-women-through-wrenches-and-car-lifts. Banks graduated from Delaware Technical Community College's automotive technology program in 2013 and quit her position at DuPont one month later.

"About," Girls Auto Clinic, accessed November 2025, https://www.girlsautoclinic.com/aboutgac. The shop opened in Upper Darby, Pennsylvania in 2017 and features transparent pricing, free monthly car care workshops, and Clutch Beauty Bar—a nail salon integrated into the repair facility.

Patrice Banks, *Girls Auto Clinic Glove Box Guide* (New York: Touchstone, 2017).

"How Patrice Banks Is Getting Women Revved Up about Auto Mechanics," ESPN, September 25, 2017, https://www.espn.com/espnw/sports/story/_/id/20795031/how-girls-auto-clinic-founder-patrice-banks-getting-women-revved-auto-mechanics; "Patrice Banks' Girls Auto Clinic

Builds a Local Army of SheCanics," The Philadelphia Citizen, July 29, 2020, https://thephiladelphiacitizen.org/shecanics-patrice-banks-girls-auto-clinic/. Within one year of opening, Banks hired five female mechanics and built a clientele that was 75% women by 2018.

Banks received media coverage in TIME, Forbes, Glamour, NPR, The Washington Post, and Oprah Magazine. Fox considered a TV pilot based on her story titled "Patty's Auto" in 2019. In 2025, she was inducted into the African American Automotive Association Hall of Fame. "Who Is Patrice Banks? Female Mechanic and CEO of Girl's Auto Clinic," The US Sun, November 22, 2024, https://www.the-sun.com/motors/12945801/patrice-banks-ceo-girls-auto-clinic/.

Women represent approximately 2% of automotive service technicians and mechanics in the United States. "Car Mechanic Demographics and Statistics [2025]: Number of Car Mechanics in the US," Zippia, January 8, 2025, https://www.zippia.com/car-mechanic-jobs/demographics/; "Automotive Service Technicians & Mechanics," Data USA, accessed November 2025, https://datausa.io/profile/soc/automotive-service-technicians-mechanics.

Chapter 3

Madam C.J. Walker

A'Lelia Bundles, *On Her Own Ground: The Life and Times of Madam C.J. Walker* (New York: Scribner, 2001). Biographical details including Walker's birth as Sarah Breedlove in 1867 to formerly enslaved parents, orphaning at age seven, marriage at fourteen, widowhood at twenty, and her development of hair care products beginning with approximately $1.50 in capital.

Bundles, *On Her Own Ground*. Walker married Charles Joseph Walker in 1906 and adopted the name Madam C.J. Walker for her business ventures.

Bundles, *On Her Own Ground*; "Madam C.J. Walker," Wikipedia, last modified September 27, 2025, https://en.wikipedia.org/wiki/Madam_C._J._Walker. Walker built a network of sales agents called "Walker Agents" who sold her products through a direct-sales model. By her death in 1919, she had become one of the first American women to become a self-made millionaire.

"Annie Malone and Madam C.J. Walker: Pioneers of the African American Beauty Industry," National Museum of African American History and Culture, October 1, 2019, https://nmaahc.si.edu/explore/stories/annie-malone-and-madam-cj-walker-pioneers-african-american-beauty-industry; "Annie Turnbo Malone," Historic Missourians, State Historical Society of Missouri, September 20, 2023, https://historicmissourians.shsmo.org/annie-turnbo-malone/. Walker worked as a sales agent for Annie Turnbo Malone before establishing her own company, learning Malone's direct-sales system before adapting it for her own business.

"Sara Blakely," Biography.com, 2024, https://www.biography.com/business-leaders/sara-blakely. Blakely famously cut the feet off her own pantyhose before developing the Spanx product line.

Chapter 4

Annie Turnbo Malone

"Annie Minerva Turnbo Pope Malone (1869–1957)," Missouri Encyclopedia, accessed November 2025, https://missouriencyclopedia.org/people/malone-annie-minerva-turnbo-pope. Biographical details including birth as the tenth of eleven children in Metropolis, Illinois, to formerly enslaved parents, early orphaning, and chronic childhood illness requiring her to leave high school before graduation.

"Annie Turnbo Malone," Historic Missourians, State Historical Society of Missouri, September 20, 2023, https://historicmissourians.shsmo.org/annie-turnbo-malone/; "Annie Minerva Turnbo Pope Malone," Missouri Encyclopedia. Malone developed "Wonderful Hair Grower" formula by 1900, moved to St. Louis in 1902 to establish the Poro Company, and opened Poro College in 1918. At its peak, the institution occupied a full city block and employed over 200 people.

"Annie Malone and Madam C.J. Walker: Pioneers of the African American Beauty Industry," National Museum of African American History and Culture, October 1, 2019, https://nmaahc.si.edu/explore/stories/annie-malone-and-madam-cj-walker-pioneers-african-american-beauty-industry. Madam C.J. Walker worked as a Poro sales agent before establishing her own company, learning Malone's direct-sales and training methods.

M. Quintana, "Annie Turnbo Malone (1869-1957)," BlackPast.org, July 30, 2025, https://blackpast.org/african-american-history/annie-turnbo-malone-1869-1957/; "Peoria's First Black Female Millionaire," Peoria Magazine, August 31, 2022, https://www.peoriamagazines.com/ibi/2022/aug/peorias-first-black-female-millionaire. Malone became one of the first Black women millionaires in America. Her company trained approximately 75,000 agents. A 1927 divorce settlement cost her $200,000. The Great Depression severely impacted her finances, and in 1951 the government seized the company for unpaid taxes. She died in 1957.

"Annie Turnbo Malone," Wikipedia, last modified September 27, 2025, https://en.wikipedia.org/wiki/Annie_Turnbo_Malone; additional biographical details from Encyclopedia.com and other general reference sources.

Chapter 5

Charis Jones

"Charis Jones," Wikipedia, accessed November 2025, https://en.wikipedia.org/wiki/Charis_Jones; "Charis Jones: Building a Jewelry Empire," Femi Magazine, accessed November 2025, https://femimagazine.com/?p=13823. Biographical details including birthdate (October 31, 1982) and Hampton University education.

"How Charis Jones Turned Her Side Hustle into an $80 Million Company," Face2Face Africa, accessed November 2025, https://face2faceafrica.com/article/how-charis-jones-turned-her-side-hustle-into-an-80-million-company; "Talking Shop," Virginia Business, accessed November 2025, https://virginiabusiness.com/talking-shop/. Charis Jones founded Sassy Jones in June 2013 as a side business while working corporate jobs, selling handcrafted jewelry from her car trunk and at trade shows. In 2016, she pivoted to livestream sales using Facebook Live from her kitchen while caring for twin infants.

Amy Feldman, "Survivors & Thrivers: 25 Small Business Standouts That Have Thrived During the Pandemic," *Forbes*, October 6, 2020, https://www.forbes.com/sites/amyfeldman/2020/10/06/survivors--thrivers/. Sassy Jones was recognized by Forbes for thriving during the 2020 pandemic, with sales reaching $1.5 million per month.

"Richmond-Based Sassy Jones Owner Wins Regional Entrepreneurial Award," *Richmond Times-Dispatch*, accessed November 2025, https://richmond.com/business/richmond-based-sassy-jones-owner-wins-regional-entrepreneurial-award/. Sassy Jones was listed on the Inc. 5000 at No. 1,903 in 2022.

"The Sassy Jones Founder on Small Business Leadership," Tory Burch Foundation, accessed November 2025, https://www.toryburchfoundation.org/resources/build-my-team/the-sassy-jones-founder-on-small-business-leadership/. Additional context on Jones's leadership approach and business growth.

D. L. Reyes, N. D. Christiansen, and R. P. Tett, "How Perceived Discrimination and Professional Rejection Sensitivity Impact Women's Career Success," *Social Psychology* 54, no. 3 (2024): 390-404, https://doi.org/10.1111/jasp.13018.

"Starting a Business without Funding: 5 Bootstrapping Strategies," Gusto Resources, June 12, 2025, https://gusto.com/resources/articles/start-business/how-to-bootstrap-business.

"Live Commerce - Statistics & Facts," Statista, 2024, https://www.statista.com/topics/8752/livestream-ecommerce/.

J. Kirtley and S. O'Mahony, "What Is a Pivot? Explaining When and How Entrepreneurial Firms Decide to Make Strategic Change and Pivot Their Business Model," *Strategic Management Journal* 44, no. 1 (2023): 197-230, https://doi.org/10.1002/smj.3131.

Chapter 6

Phoebe Robinson

"Phoebe Robinson," Wikipedia, last modified September 11, 2025, https://en.wikipedia.org/wiki/Phoebe_Robinson. Biographical details including birth (September 28, 1984, Bedford Heights, Ohio), education at Gilmour Academy and Pratt Institute, entry into stand-up comedy in 2008, creation of "Blaria" blog and live show.

"Jessica Williams (Actress)," Wikipedia, last modified September 15, 2025, https://en.wikipedia.org/wiki/Jessica_Williams_(actress). Biographical details including birth (July 31, 1989, Los Angeles County), education at Nathaniel Narbonne High School and Cal State Long Beach, and becoming The Daily Show correspondent in 2012 at age 22.

"2 Dope Queens," Wikipedia, last modified March 5, 2025, https://en.wikipedia.org/wiki/2_Dope_Queens. The podcast launched April 4, 2016 on WNYC Studios, hit #1 on iTunes in its first week, and recorded 49 main episodes plus 20 bonus episodes before concluding in November 2018.

"'2 Dope Queens' Podcast Coming to HBO," The Daily Beast, August 10, 2017, http://www.thedailybeast.com/2-dope-queens-podcast-coming-to-hbo. HBO ordered four hour-long specials to premiere in February 2018, with Phoebe Robinson and Jessica Williams as executive producers.

"Hear '2 Dope Queens' Interview Michelle Obama in Final Podcast Episode," Rolling Stone, November 14, 2018, https://www.rollingstone.com/culture/culture-news/2-dope-queens-jessica-williams-phoebe-robinson-final-episode-michelle-obama-755662/. The podcast's final episode featured Former First Lady Michelle Obama as guest.

"Phoebe Robinson Moves From '2 Dope Queens' Into Producing and Publishing," The Hollywood Reporter, accessed November 2025, https://www.hollywoodreporter.com/tv/tv-news/phoebe-robinson-moves-from-2-dope-queens-into-producing-and-publishing-4165484/; "About," Phoebe Robinson official website, accessed November 2025, https://www.phoeberobinson.com/about. Robinson's post-2 Dope Queens career includes New

York Times bestselling books *You Can't Touch My Hair* (2016), *Everything's Trash, But It's Okay* (2018), and *Please Don't Sit on My Bed in Your Outside Clothes* (2021); founding Tiny Reparations Books publishing imprint in partnership with Plume/Penguin Random House (2020); *Doing the Most* interview show on Comedy Central (2021); *Everything's Trash* TV series on Freeform (2022); and a first-look TV deal with Sony Pictures Television (2024).

Chapter 7

Viola Davis

"Viola Davis," Wikipedia, last modified September 18, 2025, https://en.wikipedia.org/wiki/Viola_Davis. Biographical information including birth (August 11, 1965) on Singleton Plantation in St. Matthews, South Carolina, education at Rhode Island College and Juilliard School (1989-1993), early career struggles including earning $518 for one day's work in *The Substance of Fire* (1996), and steady work in theater and small film/TV roles throughout the 1990s and 2000s.

"Looking Back on the Career of Actress Viola Davis, Who Was Born on an SC Plantation Where She Recently Moved Her Family," *Post and Courier*, accessed November 2025, https://www.postandcourier.com/charleston_scene/looking-back-on-the-career-of-actress-viola-davis-who-was-born-on-an-sc-plantation-where-she-was-born-in-sc/article_6138a0b3-3599-42e9-9734-6be354e17440.html. Details about Davis's birth on Singleton Plantation, her family's sharecropping background, and childhood poverty.

"How Tony, Emmy, and Oscar Winner Viola Davis Went from Juilliard Grad to Groundbreaking Actor," Playbill, February 24, 2020, https://www.playbill.com/article/emmys-2017-how-tony-emmy-and-oscar-winner-viola-davis-went-from-juilliard-grad-to-groundbreaking-actor. Davis was accepted to Juilliard on the spot as one of 14 students out of 2,500 applicants, receiving a full scholarship from 1989-1993.

Roger Ebert, "Doubt Movie Review," RogerEbert.com, December 10, 2008, https://www.rogerebert.com/reviews/doubt-2008. Ebert's review containing the quote: "It lasts about 10 minutes, but it is the emotional heart and soul of Doubt, and if Viola Davis isn't nominated by the Academy, an injustice will have been done."

"List of Awards and Nominations Received by Viola Davis," Wikipedia, last modified 2025, https://en.wikipedia.org/wiki/List_of_awards_and_nominations_received_by_Viola_Davis. Comprehensive documentation of Davis's awards including two Tony Awards, an Emmy (2015), Oscar win for *Fences* (2016), and Grammy for audiobook of *Finding Me* (2022).

"Only 22 People Had Ever Accomplished This Feat. Now, Viola Davis Joins the Club," *The Washington Post*, September 10, 2023, https://www.washingtonpost.com/lifestyle/style/forget-the-egot-only-22-people-have-accomplished-this-more-impressive-feat/2017/02/21/bdd85036-d742-11e6-9f9f-5cdb4b7f8dd7_story.html. Davis achieved EGOT status (Emmy, Grammy, Oscar, Tony) in 2022, becoming one of the few performers in history to win all four major entertainment awards.

Chapter 8

Janice Bryant Howroyd

"Janice Bryant Howroyd," Wikipedia, last modified September 30, 2025, https://en.wikipedia.org/wiki/Janice_Bryant_Howroyd. Biographical details including birth

(September 1, 1952, Tarboro, North Carolina), fourth of eleven children, experience with segregation and hostile integration at her high school, father's lesson about proving racist teacher wrong through results.

"How Janice Bryant Howroyd Turned a $900 Loan from Her Mom Into a Billion-Dollar Business," CNBC, April 20, 2018, https://www.cnbc.com/2018/04/20/janice-bryant-howroyd-used-1500-to-start-a-billion-dollar-business.html. Howroyd started ACT-1 (later ActOne Group) in 1978 with $1,500 ($900 borrowed from her mother plus $600 she had saved), operating from the front of a Beverly Hills rug store with only a telephone and phone book.

"North Carolina A&T State University," Wikipedia, last modified October 28, 2025, https://en.wikipedia.org/wiki/North_Carolina_A&T_State_University. Howroyd earned a full scholarship and graduated with a degree in English from North Carolina A&T State University (1970-1974).

"This Black Woman's Business Is on the Cusp of $3 Billion in Revenues. Here's How She Did It," *Black Enterprise*, June 20, 2023, https://www.blackenterprise.com/black-woman-business-3-billion-revenues/. ActOne Group surpassed $1 billion in annual revenue in 2018, making Howroyd the first African American woman to own and operate a company with over $1 billion in revenue. By 2021, the company reported over $3 billion in annual revenue.

"ActOne Group Founder Janice Bryant Howroyd: Never Compromise Your Values in a Quest to Succeed," *Harvard Business Review*, February 2, 2023, https://hbr.org/2023/02/actone-group-founder-janice-bryant-howroyd-never-compromise-your-values-in-a-quest-to-succeed. Howroyd's negotiation philosophy emphasizing data-driven value demonstration, her "candidate at the center of our universe" approach, money-back guarantee strategy, and development of proprietary "Acceleration" technology for detailed employee reporting.

"About ActOne Group," ActOne Group, accessed November 2025, https://www.actonegroup.com/about.aspx; "About," Ask JBH, accessed November 2025, https://askjbh.com/about/. The ActOne Group operates in 19 countries with over 17,000 clients worldwide. In July 2025, ActOne launched "Assembly Orchestration," an AI-enabled process automation platform. Howroyd hosts the "Ask JBH" podcast and serves on multiple boards including Harvard Women's Leadership Board, United Way Worldwide, and North Carolina A&T State University Board of Trustees.

Chapter 9

Cathy Hughes

"Cathy Hughes," Wikipedia, last modified August 31, 2025, https://en.wikipedia.org/wiki/Cathy_Hughes. Biographical information including birth as Catherine Elizabeth Woods in 1947 in Logan Fontenelle Housing Projects, Omaha, Nebraska; father William Alfred Woods was first African American to earn accounting degree from Creighton University; pregnant at 16 and kicked out by mother; first radio job at KOWH in Omaha (1969); moved to Washington, D.C. to work at Howard University's WHUR-FM, becoming General Sales Manager by 1973 and VP/General Manager by 1975 (first woman to hold that position).

"Company History," Urban One, accessed November 2025, https://urban1.com/company/. In 1980, after 32 commercial lending officers said "no," Hughes secured financing to purchase WOL-AM radio station in Washington, D.C. when the 33rd loan officer said "yes."

"International Sweethearts of Rhythm," Smithsonian Institution, accessed November 2025, https://www.si.edu/spotlight/international-sweethearts-of-rhythm. Cathy's mother, Helen Woods, played trombone with the International Sweethearts of Rhythm, an all-women jazz band.

"Cathy Hughes Founded Radio One While Raising Her Son Solo," ESME, May 31, 2017, https://esme.com/single-moms/solo-mom-in-the-spotlight/cathy-hughes-promise-kept. Hughes lived in the radio station with her young son Alfred after buying WOL-AM, using the station's facilities while building the business.

"Learn About Cathy Hughes, Urban One Founder & First African-American Woman to Chair a Publicly-Traded Company," Maryland Women's Business Center, February 20, 2019, https://marylandwbc.org/2019-aahm-profile3/. Hughes founded Radio One, which went public in 1999, making her the first African American woman to chair a publicly traded corporation. The company later became Urban One and includes TV One.

Chapter 10

Simone Biles

"Simone Biles," Wikipedia, accessed November 2025, https://en.wikipedia.org/wiki/Simone_Biles; "Simone Biles: Meet the Athlete," NBC Olympics, accessed November 2025, https://www.nbcolympics.com/news/simone-biles-meet-athlete; "What Happened to Simone Biles at Tokyo Olympics," Overland IOP, accessed November 2025, https://overlandiop.com/what-happened-to-simone-biles-at-tokyo-olympics/; "Simone Biles Returns with US Classic Overall Win," Deutsche Welle, August 2023, https://www.dw.com/en/gymnastics-simone-biles-returns-with-us-classic-overall-win/a-66450842. Biographical information including birth in Columbus, Ohio to mother Shannon Biles who struggled with addiction; foster care; adoption by grandparents Ron and Nellie Biles at age 3; move to Spring, Texas; ADHD diagnosis at age 6 and Ritalin prescription ("I've taken medicine for ADHD since I was a kid"); discovery of gymnastics on daycare field trip at age 6 where she spontaneously copied older gymnasts; training under Coach Aimee Boorman at Bannon's Gymnastix; 2013 breakdown at U.S. Classic followed by comeback to win World Championships; 2016 Rio Olympics (4 gold medals, 1 bronze); becoming the most decorated gymnast in history; 2018 revelation of abuse by Larry Nassar; 2023 return to competition at age 26 winning her 8th national all-around title, breaking a 90-year record.

S. Gregory, "Simone Biles Withdraws: A Reminder That Even Stars Need to Protect Mental Health," CNN, July 27, 2021, https://www.cnn.com/2021/07/27/opinions/simone-biles-tokyo-olympics-gymnastics-pressure-gregory. Biles withdrew from multiple events at the 2021 Tokyo Olympics after experiencing "the twisties" (loss of spatial awareness mid-air), prioritizing her mental health and physical safety over competition. She later returned to compete on balance beam and won bronze.

"Simone Biles Testimony on Larry Nassar Abuse Investigation [Opening Statement Transcript]," Senate Judiciary Committee, September 15, 2021, https://www.rev.com/transcript-editor/shared/simone-biles-testimony-on-larry-nassar-abuse-investigation-opening-statement-transcript. Biles testified before Congress about being abused by team doctor Larry Nassar and criticized USA Gymnastics and other organizations for failing to protect athletes.

R. Sanchez, "Simone Biles 'Shocked' and 'Honored' After Receiving Presidential Medal of Freedom," *Harper's Bazaar*, July 8, 2022, https://www.harpersbazaar.com/celebrity/latest/a40556047/simone-biles-youngest-person-presidential-medal-of-freedom/. In 2022, President Biden awarded Biles the Presidential Medal of Freedom, the nation's highest civilian honor.

"Paris 2024 Olympics Gymnastics: Simone Biles, All Medals, and Awards - Complete List," Olympics.com, 2024, https://www.olympics.com/en/news/simone-biles-all-titles-records-and-medals-complete-list-paris-2024. At the 2024 Paris Olympics, Biles won three gold medals and one silver, bringing her total Olympic medal count to 11 (7 gold, 2 silver, 2 bronze)—the most for any American gymnast in history.

Chapter 11

Olamide Olowe

"Olamide Olowe: The Gen Z CEO Is Our Inspiration of the Week," The Brief Network, May 4, 2025, https://thebriefnetwork.com/2025/05/04/olamide-olowe-the-gen-z-ceo-is-our-inspiration-of-the-week/; "Meet Topicals Skincare Co-Founders Olamide Olowe and Claudia Teng," CNBC, August 11, 2020, https://www.cnbc.com/2020/08/11/meet-topicals-skincare-co-founders-olamide-olowe-and-claudia-teng.html; Whole Woman Network, accessed November 2025, https://wholewomannetwork.org/tag/olamide-olowe/. Olamide Olowe was born October 27, 1997, to Nigerian immigrant parents; her father was a doctor. She struggled with chronic skin conditions including hyperpigmentation and post-barbae folliculitis. She was a Division I track and field athlete at UCLA, where she co-founded SheaGIRL (a SheaMoisture subsidiary) while studying Political Science and Entrepreneurship, graduating in 2019. Claudia Teng, born 1997, is Asian-American and struggled with severe eczema, hiding her topical steroid treatments. She studied Gender and Women's Studies at UC Berkeley while pursuing pre-med and conducting dermatology research. Olowe and Teng met in 2019 through a mutual friend and bonded over their shared experiences with chronic skin conditions and frustration with the beauty industry.

"How Topicals Became Sephora's Fastest-Growing Skincare Brand in Just 2 Years," Sourcify, accessed November 2025, https://www.sourcify.com/how-topicals-became-sephoras-fastest-growing-skincare-brand-in-just-2-years/; "Topicals Has Built a Rabid Fanbase by Tackling Taboo Skin Issues Head-On," Vox, October 1, 2020, https://www.vox.com/recode/2020/10/1/21497166/topicals-clinical-skin-care-bipoc-chronic-skin-conditions-building-online-community-twitter; "Olamide Olowe Talks Rejection While Building Topicals," AfroTech, accessed November 2025, https://afrotech.com/olamide-olowe-first-venture. Topicals built a waitlist of over 13,000 people before launching in August 2020 with two products: "Like Butter" and "Faded." Olowe faced over 100 investor rejections before securing funding, with investors calling the market "dormant demand" and questioning whether chronic skin conditions represented a viable market. After launch, Topicals became Sephora's fastest-growing skincare brand, with products selling out in under 48 hours when they launched on Sephora.com in March 2021.

"Topicals Founder Olamide Olowe Becomes the Youngest Black Woman to Raise $10 Million in Funding," 21Ninety, 2022, https://www.21ninety.com/topicals-founder-olamide-olowe-becomes-the-youngest-black-woman-to-raise-10-million-in-funding. In November 2022, at age 25, Olowe raised $10 million in Series A funding led by CAVU Consumer Partners, with investments from Jay-Z's Marcy Venture Partners, Gabrielle Union, and Kelly Rowland, becoming the youngest Black woman ever to raise $10 million in a single funding round.

"About Olamide Olowe: One Million-Dollar Lesson From the Founder and CEO of Topicals," AfroTech, January 2024, https://afrotech.com/topicals-founder-ceo-olamide-olowe-reveals-capital. Topicals raised another $10 million Series A round in 2024 with CAVU leading again, bringing total funding to approximately $25 million. Olowe and Topicals President Sochi Mbadugha launched holding company Cost of Doing Business (CODB) to acquire and build businesses prioritizing culture and community.

"Sephora Announces Participants for 2022 Accelerate Brand Incubator Program," Sephora Newsroom, December 10, 2021, https://newsroom.sephora.com/sephora-announces-participants-for-2022-accelerate-brand-incubator-program-with-continued-focus-on-bipoc-brand-founders/. Topicals was selected for Sephora Accelerate program, an incubator for BIPOC-owned beauty brands providing mentorship, business training, and resources designed specifically for success at Sephora.

"Black Female Founders: Black Women Get 0.64% of Venture Capital, but Data Shows They Tripled in First Half," *Fortune*, December 2, 2020, https://fortune.com/2020/12/02/black-female-founders-venture-capital-funding-vc-2020-project-diane/. Context on systemic barriers Black women founders face in securing venture capital funding, making Olowe's fundraising achievement particularly significant.

www.ingramcontent.com/pod-product-compliance
Lightning Source LLC
LaVergne TN
LVHW021818060526
838201LV00058B/3428